John Le Couteur

On the Varieties, Properties, and Classification of Wheat

John Le Couteur

On the Varieties, Properties, and Classification of Wheat

ISBN/EAN: 9783337230029

Printed in Europe, USA, Canada, Australia, Japan

Cover: Foto ©Andreas Hilbeck / pixelio.de

More available books at **www.hansebooks.com**

ON

THE VARIETIES,

PROPERTIES, AND CLASSIFICATION

OF

WHEAT.

BY

JOHN LE COUTEUR, Esq., F.R.S., F.S.A.,
CAPTAIN H.P. LATE 104TH REGIMENT;
COLONEL 1ST REGIMENT ROYAL JERSEY MILITIA; AIDE-DE-CAMP TO THE QUEEN.

"Much food is in the tillage of the poor: but there is *that* is destroyed for want of judgment."

Second Edition.

LONDON:
W. J. JOHNSON, 121, FLEET STREET, E.C.
JERSEY: C. LE FEUVRE, THE BERESFORD LIBRARY.

1872.

CONTENTS.

	PAGE
Preface	v
Critical Notices on the First Edition	vii
Specimens of Wheat in the South Kensington Exhibition	xxi
Distinctions obtained by the Author	xxiv
Dedication	xxv
Introduction	xxix
CHAPTER I.—Wheat, its Origin and Varieties	33
,, II.—Faults in Ordinary Practice	41
,, III.—On the Choice of Seed	46
,, IV.—A First Comparative Experiment	57
,, V.—On the Roots and Growth of Wheat	67
,, VI.—On the Necessity of Preserving Crops Pure	76
,, VII.—On Meal and Bread	85
,, VIII.—On Manure for Wheat	95
,, IX.—On a Change and Choice of Seed	115
,, X.—On the Tendency of Wheat to Degenerate	121
,, XI.—On the Disposition of Wheat to Sport	131
,, XII.—On the Early Habits of some Varieties	136
,, XIII.—On the Properties of some Varieties	141
,, XIV.—Classification and Names of New Varieties	145
,, XV.—On the Relative Advantages of the Drill or Broadcast System, or Thick or Thin Sowing and Lois Weedon	151
,, XVI.—Result	165
,, XVII.—Conclusion	174

DIRECTIONS TO BINDER.

PLATE I.	face 68
,, II.	,, 68
,, III.	,, 148
,, IV.	,, 149
,, V.	,, 150

PREFACE.

HAVING received several applications for a copy of this little work on "Wheat"—moreover, being invited to prepare a Second Edition—it will be my endeavour to render it as acceptable now to my brother farmers as it was originally. There can be little offered by me that is new;—the great amount of information to be gathered in the valuable Reports of the Royal Agricultural Society of England is so extensive as to almost exhaust the subject. The only merit belonging to this book may be, that it condenses the matter. How it was received with favour on its first appearance, in the year 1836, may be seen by the various notices of the volume.

CRITICAL NOTICES OF THE FIRST EDITION.

From the "SCOTSMAN," *February* 8, 1837.

This little work ("On the Varieties, Properties, and Classification of Wheat," by John Le Couteur, Esq., Colonel of the 1st Regiment of Jersey Militia, and Aide-de-Camp to the King, 1836) should be in the possession of every cultivator of wheat. We do not regard it as exaggeration to say that it will do more for the agriculture of the empire than has been effected by all the societies instituted for the purposes of agricultural improvement put together. Colonel Le Couteur has struck into the right path, and not only has exhibited that care and discrimination which alone can render the culture of wheat completely successful, but has pointed out the means by which all the *Cerealia* may be managed with the fullest benefit to the grower and to the public. To our surprise he has dedicated his work to the Central Agricultural Association of Great Britain and Ireland—an Association evidently not brought together on the principles on which our author's experiments have been founded; but for the purpose of keeping up rent unjustly, and tampering with the currency to effect that end; deeming the filling of landlords' pockets at the expense of the tenantry a fit object for legislative interference. Our author is a member of the Association; and it is astonishing that he should address it with adulation while its objects are purely selfish, and his own to bring about amelioration in the only manner that is rational—viz., by selecting and improving the best varieties of corn, and cultivating them in the most economical manner.

But to proceed. In our opinion Colonel Le Couteur's labours place him in a higher position than any one who has preceded him in agricultural experiment. His attention to the subject of Wheat was arrested by Professor La Gasca, of Madrid, who pointed out to him that no fewer than fourteen sorts were growing promiscuously in his field at

Belle Vue. These he proceeded to separate and to cultivate. "It is," says he, "to the prosecution of these researches, after five years of close application, that I desire to call the attention of the agricultural world." "The great first principle I wish to advocate is the proper adaptation of varieties of wheat to the various soils and climates, since it is the suitableness of each sort to each soil that will enable the farmer to pay the rent of his land, by sowing one variety where he would be unable to do so by attempting to grow another of a seemingly better sort. If this end can be obtained, the object I have had in view will be realized. The farmer will be placed in a better situation than he is in now; the productiveness of the soil will be enormously increased, inasmuch as many unproductive lands may be made to grow wheat suited to them, under a proper rotation of cropping and clean husbandry. This last I hold to be indispensable, under all circumstances."

In the first chapter he quotes Columella, who wrote in the first century, and Gerard's "Herbal," published in the 17th, to show that many varieties of wheat have been long known, as well as the adaptation of different sorts to different soils—a subject not yet sufficiently attended to. Our author justly remarks that "modern writers have merely designated a number of varieties, but no attempt appears to have ever been made to class them correctly, or to ascertain their relative values by comparison." This has been our author's object, and he has done wonders in effecting it. It is remarked by Colonel Le Couteur that the unequal ripening of corn is owing solely to a mixture of varieties; and it is of the utmost importance to have every plant in a field of one sort of corn. He notices several practical matters in reference to the management of the soil intended for wheat, and his remarks are well worthy of attention. He has made experiments with the view to ascertain the baking qualities of different varieties, and treats on the subject of manure and of the changing of seed. This last practice, he thinks, proceeds on an erroneous principle, and he suggests another mode of proceeding, which also merits attention from the farmer. The observations on degeneration and sporting, and on the habits of varieties, are important. There are likewise some well-founded remarks on the relative advantages of drill and broadcast sowing.

While we strongly recommend the careful perusal of this valuable little volume to every one engaged in raising corn, we cannot help lamenting that a man of Colonel Le Couteur's acuteness should imagine that legislative interference can relieve agricultural distress when it arrives. This is the more surprising, when we find him actually pointing out one of the best remedies for it in his instructive experiments—viz., a mode of obtaining crops, abundant and of fine quality, at the least expense. We venture to say that the farmer will never feel comfortable until his landlord shall agree to share with him both prosperity and distress. The writer of these remarks, himself a landlord, saw this long since; and having brought the tenants on his own lands (with some difficulty, it is true) to understand the subject, and to see the propriety of mutual gain or loss being insured by regulating rent by prices, he has had the high satisfaction of seeing his tenants not only contented, but anxiously desiring high prices, that they might pay him better rent. Not only has he that satisfaction, but every one of them, feeling himself secure from loss, has gone on with activity to execute extensive improvements and to reclaim waste-land; thus amply compensating to their landlord any imaginary loss which short-sighted persons are apt to dread.

From the " PLYMOUTH NEWS*," January 7th*, 1837.

WHEAT.—IMPORTANT TO FARMERS.—Circumstances led Colonel Le Couteur, of Jersey, to make a collection of wheats; and in the course of five years' close attention and research, it increased to upwards of 150 sorts, among which he found some that throve better than others in the particular soils and situations adapted to each all over the kingdom. ONE EAR of a SUPERIOR variety, SOWN GRAIN BY GRAIN, and suffered TO TILLER apart, yielded 4 lbs. 4 oz. of wheat; while another, of an inferior sort, treated in the same manner, produced but 1 lb. 10 oz., showing the vast importance of selecting the MOST PRODUCTIVE and FARINACEOUS sorts of seed, the profit of sowing one sort and the loss resulting from the other being manifest. Five years since the Colonel found no less than 80 distinct sorts of wheat growing in a nursery-garden in Jersey, some of which were seven feet high, some only four, the ears of some being three, of others six inches long; the nature of which was explained to him by Professor La Gasca, who first called his attention to the subject. On requesting the Professor to visit some fields of his which he imagined to be cropped with as pure and unmixed wheat as those of his neighbours, to his dismay the Professor drew from them no less than twenty-three distinct varieties—some white wheat, some red, some liver-coloured, and some spring wheat, some DEAD RIPE, the corn shaking out, some RIPE, some HALF RIPE, some in a MILKY STATE, and some GREEN; from all of which he was convinced that "no crop IN THAT STATE could either produce the greatest weight of corn, give the largest quantity of flour, or make the best or lightest bread, such as would be produced from a field in an equal and perfect state of ripeness." The Colonel then selected fourteen of the best and most productive sorts of wheat, which he cultivated with great care and success, showing the advantages of such care and selection, and the immense benefit arising from them both to individuals and the nation. These, and a multitude of other equally interesting and important particulars, are contained in a little work, lately published by Colonel Le Couteur, "On the Varieties, Properties, and Classification of Wheat," which we cannot too strongly recommend to the attention of our agricultural readers.

From the "STAR."

The Review of Colonel Le Couteur's work, "On the Properties and Classification of Wheat," affords sufficient insight into the subject to make us wish to possess the book itself. The importance of selecting healthy and prolific seed is made manifest, and we are told that Colonel Le Couteur has practically proved the soundness of his system, by raising four, five, and even six quarters of wheat per acre, from land that formerly only averaged three quarters. This is the same thing as doubling the surface of an estate, and we cordially recommend his principles to all agriculturists, and particularly to the farmers of Guernsey. If they want to make money, here the secret is explained, for they may now find Aladdin's lamp, if they choose to read.

From the "GUERNSEY STAR."

Many interesting and important subjects were discussed, and particularly, for the present season, as to the causes and cure of smut in wheat, &c. Colonel Le Couteur's pamphlet, "On the Varieties, Properties, and Classification of Wheat," is the first book purchased by the Ashbocking Association, and arrangements are making for raising a fund to purchase other books on Agriculture. The Ashbocking Farmers' Club, therefore, promises to become extremely useful, and if similar clubs were established in every district, acting in concert by deputation in aid of the Central Society in London *at a reduced rate of subscription to that body*, as will be proposed at the general committee of the latter society in December next—namely, 3*l*. annually—much good might arise, provided one general union of the whole agricultural body of the United Kingdom could be formed and confined purely to *agricultural improvement and protection*. The latter object would be accomplished by watching over the deliberations of Parliament through the Central Society in London, which is already distinguished by numerous and powerful supporters in both Houses of Parliament presiding at the head of it. For such a union would always find its best interests promoted by *never touching the discordant string of politics* till the moment arrived when it may be necessary to exert the influence of a general body to stop measures injurious to the whole community of producers and consumers at home. A union like this would again restore the landed interests to its just position in the empire, and be productive of incalculable advantages to the country. The greatest praise, therefore, is due to Mr. Charles Poppy, the excellent Chairman of the Farmers' Club at Ashbocking, and to all the members of it, collectively and individually, for an example that may be followed most beneficially in the rural districts, especially seeing that among the *first-fruits* of the Central Society in London *the gradual repeal of the malt-tax* is not unlikely to result.

At the date of our last the state of the crops gave promise of part reaching maturity by the end of August, but dropping and cloudy weather has retarded the ripening progress, and only a few fields of barley have as yet been cut down. Much, however, on early lands and where early sown, may be cut down in course of next week. The Belle Vue Talavera wheat, a very early and fine variety from the famous Colonel Le Couteur, Jersey, has been cut down fully ripe, and promises to be a good variety for spring sowing.—*Perthshire Local Paper*, September 8, 1839.

From the "JERSEY BRITISH PRESS," *February*, 1837.

The following complimentary notice of the work on Wheat, by the Honorary Secretary to the Agricultural Department of our Agricultural and Horticultural Society, has lately appeared in a distinguished

Edinburgh newspaper, the *Scotsman*. We may here briefly observe, that though the able reviewer of the work has done it ample justice for originality of conception, and any intrinsic merit it may possess, yet in treating the subject he appears to have overlooked the sound advice offered to the Central Agricultural Society of Great Britain and Ireland, in the concluding statement, "showing the advantages to be conferred on the agricultural interests generally by the establishment of an experimental farm in the immediate vicinity of London," written by Colonel Le Couteur, in December, 1835, long before the appointment of the second Select Committee of the House of Commons on Agriculture, where it was distinctly shown that the agriculturists must "rather trust to their own exertions than hope for any relief from the Legislature, which has so recently been occupied in making twelve thousand nine hundred and three questions, which, with the replies, occupy 617 pages, on the causes of agricultural distress. It appears, therefore, doubtful whether any legislative enactment could speedily relieve those heavy burdens which unhappily oppress agriculturists; the various interests of the State requiring to be so nicely balanced and adjusted, and being so closely interwoven, that any concession made to one might be detrimental to the others." The true means of obtaining which he shows in the following terms : " But the first and most legitimate step towards relieving the farming interest is to unite in one great body, steadily to examine all the bearings of the question which affect its interests ; not by merely calling out for help, like the carman in the fable, but by putting a shoulder to the wheel—by rousing energies that have long lain dormant; by an inquiry into each other's wants ; by the introduction of new plants congenial to the soil; by the application of capital to the growth of new crops ; by a rapid interchange of commodities, the harbinger to prosperity, which steam communication and railways will facilitate ; by pointing out to the farmer that the soil is not cultivated to its extent ; by clearly exposing that if he grows a crop of weeds in addition to the crop he may have put into the ground, it is just so much produce taken from his capital and given to waste."

This holds good with pasture as well as crops ; if nothing but nutritious herbage were grown, another head of cattle would be reared on every farm in the kingdom, and the increase of stock would be in proportion to the superior culture of the soil.

Now, had the gallant author been gifted with the spirit of prophecy, he could not have more distinctly foretold that the labours of the last Committee of the House of Commons would be a dead lett

Politics have been studiously avoided in this little work, which is confined to the consideration of the best interests of the farmer, the successful growth of that product which is the sheet anchor of his husbandry; and he emphatically calls on all those whose education and habits must lead them fully to appreciate the paramount im_ portance of a perfect system of agriculture in the British Empire, to sacrifice all party views on the altar of their country, and to unite for the common interest on the only neutral ground which presents itself—an experimental farm, devoted to the scientific inquiry of what products are best fitted for the various soils and climates in the empire.

It is with satisfaction we observe that the Society of Arts have given consideration to the subject, and that samples of twenty-four varieties of wheat raised by the Colonel were exhibited at their last meeting.

Colonel Le Couteur has recently received a most acceptable addition to his collection of wheats, through the polite attention of Mr. Loudon, the scientific and enlightened author of the Encyclopædia of Agriculture, Horticulture, and other works important to the rural arts. A magnificent collection of the varieties cultivated in France, arranged by Monsieur Vilmorin, including all those in the *Maison Rustique*, and presented by him to Mr. Loudon, were handsomely offered by that gentleman to Colonel Le Couteur, "as being the person more likely to estimate their merit and make them known than any other individual he was aware of." This augments the collection to upwards of two hundred varieties, including wheats from every quarter of the globe, which no doubt will all be submitted to close and inductive experiments.

MR. LEWIN'S REPORT ON MR. BROWN'S WHEAT.

In a former number it was noticed that Mr. Brown had sent to Mr. John Lewin, of Wickham Market, a sack of his Chevalier Ten-rowed Prolific Wheat, to be tried against Mr. Lewin's *Eclipse* Wheat. Mr. Lewin declines saying anything in praise of his own wheat, further than that both wheats make as good bread as can be obtained; in proof of which, he has sent up to the Central Society a few small loaves of bread made with each wheat. These loaves have been shown to good judges, and pronounced to be as fine as can be made. Mr. Lewin's report is to the following effect :—

"Wickham Market, Suffolk, Oct. 28, 1837.

"Dear Sir,—I received your sack of Chevalier Wheat of 260 lbs. on the 25th, and the produce is as under :—

156 lbs. superfine flour (White's) making	203½ lbs. bread.
28 lbs. seconds	37 ditto
20 lbs. middlings	
16 lbs. fine pollard	240¾ lbs.
20 lbs. coarse ditto	
12 lbs. bran	
8 lbs. loss in grinding and dressing	
260 lbs.	

"This 240½ lbs. of bread from the above quantity of flour is at the rate of 370 lbs., or 92½ four-pound loaves, from a sack of flour of 280 lbs. It is a matter of opinion as to mixing with other flour ; some persons would, others would not. *All produce partakes in some degree of the nature of the soil that produces it;* for instance, my farm and the lands generally around me are good loamy or mixed soil ; from which a sack of superfine flour will produce about 92 four-pound loaves on the average ; sandy weak soils about 90, and strong clay soils from 93 to 95 loaves, but not generally so showy or handsome.

"I have sent you a few small loaves, which I considered would be better than one large one, for show, convenience, and distribution among your friends, if you wish it, and you will see the quality is as good as can be made.—I am, dear Sir, very truly yours,

"JOHN LEWIN.

"To Mr. Brown, 46, Cheapside."

In order that the value of Mr. Brown's Chevalier Wheat, as well as the Eclipse Wheat grown by Mr. Lewin, both being as good as can be produced, may be fairly appreciated, it will be more satisfactory, probably, to compare them against No. 8, the best of 14 different varieties tried by Colonel Le Couteur, the results of which are given in a tabular form in his valuable work, "On the Properties and Classification of Wheat," page 63.

At page 62 Colonel Le Couteur observes, " No. 8, a downy variety, was still more productive than No. 1, as 55 grains produced 4 lbs. 4 oz. of wheat and 3 lbs. 13 oz. of straw, its average of tillers being 11 ; the straw of a fine colour, and the sample very beautiful, though scarcely so fine or thin-skinned as No. 1. This produced nearly three times as much corn as No. 14, and a third more straw." Again, page 66, "It must be obvious from the tables I exhibit, that a farmer who would sow No. 14 on a soil which would equally suit No. 8 might be unable to pay his rent, whereas had he happened to have sown No. 8 he would have had nearly three times more wheat and a third more straw."

Again, page 91, "From a downy or hoary variety (No. 8) 18 pounds of flour, with half a pint of yeast, five quarts and a pint of water, and one ounce of salt, made *twenty-six pounds* of beautiful light white bread.'"

"From a Dantzic wheat flour the same quantity, with the same proportion of yeast, salt, and water, made *twenty-four pounds and a half* of *very* white bread, similar to French bread.

"The same weight of spring wheat flour made *twenty-four pounds* of inferior brownish bread.

"The same weight of Rostock and Dantzic flour from wheat grown in the Baltic, made only *twenty-three pounds* of bread, very light and good; but not so white by many shades, or well flavoured, as that made from the two first varieties of home growth.

"These experiments having been made in my own presence, may be relied on. The dough was worked in the French mode, not pushed down, turned and worked with closed hands, but drawn up into long strings and repeatedly lifted, in order to expose it to the action of the air as much as possible; which tends greatly to improve the bread, by rendering it more light and easy of digestion.

"The superiority of the meal of the hoary variety of wheat, which furnished three pounds more bread on a baking of 18 pounds of flour, or an *increase of one-sixth over the Dantzic and Rostock*, which was also a very fine sample of flour, is thus clearly established.

"It is said in the article 'Baking,' in the second volume of the 'Encyclopædia Britannica,' that a sack of flour weighing 280 lbs., and containing five bushels, is supposed capable of being baked into 80 loaves, in the Act of Parliament regulating the assize of bread. According to this estimate, one-fifth of the loaf consists of water and salt, the remaining four-fifths of flour. But the fact is, that the number of quartern loaves that can be made from a sack of flour depends entirely on the goodness of that article. Good flour requires more water than bad, and old flour than new. Sometimes 82, 83, and even 86 loaves may be made out of a sack; sometimes scarcely 80.

"Now, assuming these data to be correct, the results I have obtained prove that the hoary wheat, No. 8, will afford flour that will make *ninety-three quartern loaves in each sack*, being a superiority of 10 loaves on each sack, taking the medium number 83 ; and this, be it observed, without adulteration, the pure home-made bread unmixed with alum to whiten it, or potato meal to moisten it. This superiority, be it further observed, is over a good quality of flour, or inferior red wheat, both of which I shall indicate hereafter."

Thus it appears that Mr. Lewin's Eclipse and Mr. Brown's Chevalier Ten-rowed Prolific Wheat will make 92½ loaves out of one sack, which, as compared with Colonel Le Couteur's No. 8 downy hoary wheat,* is only *half a loaf* less in produce of bread in a sack than the latter ; and that each of these wheats are superior to the Dantzic. It may be observed, that when a respectable farmer in Essex, in his examination before the Committee of the House of Commons on the state of Agriculture in 1836, was asked whether he was aware that some of the Essex wheats were equal to the present Dantzic wheat, he replied, " I do not think that any wheat in produce is equal to the Dantzic wheat. I do not consider that it ever produced so much money." It appears, however, that both Mr. Lewin and Mr. Brown have produced wheat in East and West Suffolk even superior in produce to the Dantzic variety tried by Colonel Le Couteur ; thus proving that English farmers CAN render our native soil not only profitable to themselves, but quite equal to supply the wants of the community at home, without sending abroad for bread to eat.

From the "MARK LANE EXPRESS," *December* 26, 1837.

Colonel Le Couteur, of the 1st Regiment Royal Jersey Militia, has recently published a little work that proves the writer to have made, and to be making, a most exemplary use of the happy interruption of war, and to be promoting, like an excellent citizen, the arts of peace and the means of internal support and strength. The work is " On the Varieties, Properties, and Classification of Wheat ;" and the details are the results of the writer's own experiments on his own property. Circumstances led him to make a collection of wheats ; and, in

---

* A sample of No. 8 was probably among the varieties of wheat exhibited to the Central Society by Colonel Le Couteur in 1836 ; but these had been removed before Mr. Brown's samples were compared, and a few others subsequently left, representing a variety of excellent quality.

the course of five years' close attention and research, it increased to upwards of 150 sorts. To show the importance of attending to the varieties and properties of wheat, Colonel Le Couteur mentions that among these varieties there are some that will thrive better than others, in the particular soils and situations adapted to each, all over the kingdom; that one ear of a superior variety, sowed grain by grain, and suffered to tiller apart, produced 4 lbs. 4 oz. of wheat; whereas another ear, of an inferior sort, treated in the same manner, produced only 1 lb. 10 oz.—a proof of the paramount importance of selecting the most productive and farinaceous sorts of seed, the profit of sowing one sort and the loss resulting from the other being manifest. The writer remarks that his attention was directed to this important subject by Professor La Gasca, Curator of the Royal Gardens at Madrid; that five years since he accidentally saw about 80 distinct sorts of wheat growing in a nursery-garden in Jersey, some seven feet high, some only four, the ears of some being three, others six inches long; and that the Professor explained their nature to him. He requested the Professor to visit his crops, considering them to be as pure and unmixed as those of his neighbours. To the writer's dismay, the Professor drew from three fields 23 sorts—some white wheat, some red, some liver-coloured, some spring wheat, some dead ripe, the corn shaking out, some ripe, some half so, some in a milky state, and some green. He thereupon became convinced that "no crop in that state could either produce the greatest weight of corn, give the largest quantity of flour, or make the best or lightest bread, such as would be produced from a field in an equal and perfect state of ripeness." He then selected the best and most productive sorts of wheat, and secured 14 sorts, which he afterwards cultivated with great care and success, showing the great profit resulting from this care and selection, and arguing on the immense consequences to the country if attention to this subject could be made a national object. The modes by which Colonel Le Couteur proceeded and succeeded occupy the remaining portions of the volume; and the importance of the work may be estimated when the author calculated that the successful application of his views and plans would enable this country profitably to grow far more wheat than could be consumed by many more millions of inhabitants than at present throng its isles. The interest and utility of such a publication are, therefore, too obvious to require further comment, while the author's meritorious studies cannot be too highly praised.

From the "FARMER'S CABINET" *(Philadelphia), August* 15*th,* 1838.

TO THE EDITOR OF THE "FARMER'S CABINET."

"Philadelphia, 2nd June, 1838.

"Dear Sir,—Last fall I obtained from London Le Couteur's treatise on Wheat, which having read, I am convinced it ought to be laid before the agriculturists of the United States. At first I intended to reprint the book entire, and offer it for sale, but finding myself too much engaged to attend to the republication, I send it herewith to you, that it may find its way to the wheat-growers, through the columns of the 'Cabinet,' provided you deem it an eligible subject for your useful paper.

"Deeming, as I always have, the improvement of the soil and of the mind the most important of the interests of my country, I take great pleasure in thus contributing my mite to the former of these grand objects, whilst, as you know, I daily devote my time and humble powers to the advancement of the latter, in the preparation of a portion of her young citizens for future usefulness.—Your friend,

"J. J. HITCHCOCK."

We take great pleasure in availing ourselves of the opportunity offered us by the politeness of Mr. Hitchcock, of laying before our readers the valuable treatise on Wheat, referred to in the above letter. The work, since it has been placed in our hands, has been examined by several judicious and intelligent individuals, among whom were two eminent wheat-growers; they all agreed as to its great merit, and united in recommending its republication. This we could not do conveniently in a separate form, and as it was deemed advisable to give it as extensive a circulation as possible, and as the subject is one in which all our readers are interested, we resolved to republish it in the present volume of the "Farmer's Cabinet."

We learn from the dedication of this volume that Mr. Le Couteur's collection consisted of 150 sorts. Of course some would thrive better than others in the particular soils and situations adapted to each. One ear of a superior variety which he sowed grain by grain, and suffered to tiller apart, produced 4 lbs. 4 oz. of wheat; whereas another ear of an inferior sort, treated in the same manner, produced only 1 lb. 10 oz.—a proof that it is of paramount importance to select the most productive and farinaceous sorts for seed. It is, therefore, obvious that a farmer who would have sown his entire crop with the last-named variety would have lost much, whereas the superior variety would have obtained him a large profit. Wheat-growers will, we trust, bear this always in mind.

The facts given in the little work are the result of five successive years' researches and close application. The writer recommends that, if experiments are to be made on his suggestions, they should first be on a small scale, and consequently they are attended with no hazard. In agriculture the results of experiments are necessarily tedious.

The great first principle which our author endeavours to advocate is the proper adaptation of varieties of wheat to the various soils and climate, since it is the suitableness of each sort to each soil that will enable the farmer to reap a profit by sowing one variety when he would be unable to do so by attempting to grow another of a seemingly better sort.

*From the "*GUERNSEY STAR*,"* 1838.

Since the publication of Colonel Le Couteur's (of Jersey) valuable pamphlet on the cultivation of Wheat, the agriculturists of that island, availing themselves of his suggestions, have so considerably increased the value of their produce, that Jersey wheat is now selling for five shillings per quarter more than Guernsey wheat. Every one acknowledges the great benefit this island has derived from the Agricultural and Horticultural Associations, but we think the former have now open to them a wider field of usefulness. Let them extend to corn some prizes similar to those they give to the best breed of horned cattle. The export of cows is too valuable to this island to require any comment, and there is no reason why our farmers should not create an important market for themselves in the sale of seed wheat. By sowing the same seed, as they are in the habit of doing from year to year, they deteriorate their crops, and the evil is annually becoming more serious. By adopting the recommendation of Colonel Le Couteur, there would be an increase both of quantity and quality, and the effect would be the same as if an additional number of vergees were annexed to each estate in the island. A rise of five shillings per quarter out of the same quantity of land, and without an extra cost of labour, would be an immense profit, and we earnestly hope that no prejudice in favour of old usages will blind the eyes of our farmers to their true interest. We have more than once invited attention to the practical truths established by Colonel Le Couteur, and as they have been tested by some of the most experienced farmers in England, we entertain a sanguine hope that our Agricultural Association will warmly take up the subject and encourage the classification of seed wheat by the full weight of their influence. Most certainly they could not devote their energies to a more worthy or more useful cause.

JOURNAL OF THE ENGLISH AGRICULTURAL SOCIETY.—The second number of this publication contains the principal papers for which prizes were awarded at the late meeting of the Society at Oxford, and other articles of a practical and highly useful character. The essay by Colonel Le Couteur, "On Pure and Improved Varieties of Wheat lately introduced into England," has excited very considerable attention; and although we gave a summary of the paper shortly after the prize was awarded, we are induced to insert the whole essay, as the information it contains appears to us most interesting to the agriculturist.

From "COBBETT'S REGISTER," *p.* 406 (1835).

The following very interesting article on the cultivation of "Wheat for Seed" I most earnestly recommend to my readers:—

Colonel Le Couteur has kept a most minute account of his experiments, and taken the greatest care to preserve the best sorts, and in their purity. He has in London nineteen varieties of the greatest beauty, and such as the frequenters of Mark-lane say could not be matched in England for purity. The Colonel, after three years' experience, has arrived at this conclusion, that the proper cultivation of wheat is yet unknown or unpractised.

From the "BON JARDINIER." *Paris*, 1851. "*Cériales.*"

"Blé Talavera de Belle Vue.—Ce blé a été mis en prémière ligne et repandu en Angleterre par le Colonel Le Couteur, de Jersey, auteur d'un mémoire fort remarquable sur les variétés de froment."

From DARWIN, *Vol. II.*: "ANIMALS AND PLANTS UNDER DOMESTICATION." *London.* 1868.

Another excellent observer, Colonel Le Couteur, has come to the same conclusion (as M. Tessier), but then he expressly adds, if the same seed be used, "that which is grown on land manured from the mixed one year becomes seed for land prepared with lime, and that again becomes seed for land dressed with ashes, then for land dressed with mixed manure, and so on." But this in effect is a systematic exchange of seed within the limits of the same farm.—*p.* 147.

The finest shades of difference in wheat have been discriminated and selected with almost as much care as we see in Colonel Le Couteur's works, as in the case of the higher animals; but with our cereals the process of selection has seldom, or never, been long continued.—*p.* 200.

CONTENTS OF A CASE

IN THE

SOUTH KENSINGTON MUSEUM.

LE COUTEUR, JOHN—*Belle Vue, Jersey*, Producer.

Specimens and notes of produce of some of the most approved varieties of Wheat cultivated in Great Britain or elsewhere, arranged by Colonel John Le Couteur, F.R.S., M.S.A., Aide-de-Camp to Her Majesty the Queen.

White winter wheat (Fr., *Froments blancs d'hiver;* Ger. *Winter Weizen*).

Var. No. 1. Triticum Hibernum, Hybridum Candidum, Epulonum Leucospermum of La Gasca, ex-Curator, Royal Gardens, Madrid.

1. Dantzic (Jersey). See Grain. 52 imperial bushels to the acre.
2. Chidham. 1838.—18lbs. of flour produced 26lbs. 4oz. of excellent white bread. Nature dry.
3. Berkshire.
4. Lewin's Eclipse.
5. Clutton.
6. Whittington. 1841.—27lbs. of flour produced 37lbs. of good bread, rather brown. Keeps moist.
7. Brown's Chevalier. 27lbs. produced 36lbs. 4oz. excellent white bread.
8. Canada.
9. Burrill, from Earl Spencer. 1842.—27lbs. of flour produced 36lbs. white bread.
10. Hardcastle.
11. Old Essex.
12. Pegglesham.
13. Ten-rowed Prolific.
14. Old Suffolk.
15. Earl Toham.
16. White Dantzic, Lincoln.
17. Old Lammas Prize, Devon.
18. Dantzic, Oxford.
19. Old Welsh White Lemon.
20. Mullybrack, Norfolk.
21. Pearl, Scotland.
22. French.
23. London Superior.
24. Royal Standard.
25. Baltic. 18lbs. of flour produced 23lbs. bread.
26. Kentish long.

Winter compact varieties (Fr. *Froments carrés;* Ger. *Vierzeilige Weizen*).

Var. No. 2. Trit. Hib. Album Densum, of La Gasca.

1. Jersey Pearl. 48 bushels to the acre. 18lbs. of flour produced 24lbs. of bread, white, dry nature. 1837.
2. Ducksbill, Kiel. 1836.—18lbs. of flour produced 24lbs. of bread, rather moist.

3. Britannia.
4. Buckland, Toussaint, Devon.
5. Suffolk Thickest.
6. Mazzochino, Italy.
7. Buff Surrey.
8. Chili. 1848.—27lbs. of flour produced 34lbs. 12oz. brown heavy bread. Condemned after seven years of trial, though suited to the stormy regions of the Mountains of Chili.
9. Cape of Good Hope.
10. Coturianum. Compactum, La Gasca. 58 bushels to the acre. 27lbs of flour produced 36lbs. 2oz. white bread, of a moist nature.

Var. No. 3. Elongated winter wheat (Fr. *Froments alongés*; Ger. *Weizen Verlangen*).

Trit. Hyb. Candidissimum Epulonum of La Gasca.

1. Dantzic, Jersey. See Grain, High-mixed, of commerce. 27lbs. of flour produced 35¼lbs. of excellent white bread.
2. Cape of Good Hope, longest.
3. Cape of Good Hope. 1840.—27lbs. of flour produced 37lbs. 8oz. of white moist bread.
4. Malaga.
5. Lupo, Italy.
6. Gran gentil et Rosso. This seed was seven years in the hands of Mr. Aiken, late Secretary of the Society of Arts.
7. Van Diemen's Land.
8. Crim Tartary.
9. Var. High-mixed, Dantzic.

Var. No. 4. Downy, or hoary wheat (Fr. *Veloutés*; Ger. *Wolligweizen*).

Trit. Hyb. Koeleri of La Gasca.

1. Kentish Downy. See Grain B. V. 55 bushels to the acre. 18lbs. flour produced 26lbs. of bread, excellent quality.
2. Guinea, Norfolk.
3. Turgidum.
4. Imperial Buff.
5. Tunstall rough Chaff.
6. Italian.
7. Coturiunum Confertum of La Gasca.
8. Red-grained.
9. Chili, 1850. To be tried.
10. Jersey, 20lbs. 6oz. of this flour, and 6lbs. 10oz. of bran, produced 39lbs. 1oz. of good bread, second quality.

Var. No. 5. Red wheats (Fr. *Froments Rouges*; Ger. *Roth Weizen*). Trit Hib. Glabrum Rufum of La Gasca.

1. Golden Drop. See Grain.
2. Red Hair Welsh.
3. Rattling Jack.
4. Old Red Norfolk.
5. New Red Norfolk.
6. Old Red Lammas.
7. Britannia.
8. Red Chaff Dantzic.
9. Blood-red Scotch.
10. Syer's.
11. York Square-headed.
12. Copdock.
13. Golden Prolific.
14. Red Burrill.
15. Essex.
16. Prolific.
17. Sark, very hardy.
18. White Golden Drop.
19. Gigantic.
20. Grand Rubella.
21. Compact Red.
22. Kiel.
23. Cape of Good Hope. 1840.—18lbs. of flour produced 26lbs. 6oz. of brown bread, of dry nature.
24. Pale red Cape.

Var. No. 6. Spring Wheats (Fr. *Bleds de Mars Trémois;* Ger. *Springen Weizen).* Triticum Æstivum Candidum Epulonum of La Gasca. Beardless *(Sans barbes).*

1. Belle Vue Talavera (Col. Le Couteur's Seedling). See Grain. 1838. 52 bushels to the acre. 1841.--27lbs. of flour produced 35lbs. 14oz. bread of the finest quality.
2. Old proved Talavera, Spain.
3. Malaga.
4. Italian.

5. Cape White. 1840. —27lbs. flour produced 37¼lbs. white moist bread.
6. Mummy. Tombs of the Kings of Thebes. Sir Gardner Wilkinson.' Raised at Belle Vue from one ear sent by M. Tupper, Esq. 1846.—27lbs. flour produced 35lbs. bread. Very light, white, superior.

Var. No. 7. Bearded (Fr. *Bleds trémois barbus;* Ger. *Bartweizen).*

1. White Lily (Jersey). See Grain. 27lbs. flour produced 38½lbs. bread. Moist, white, superior.
2. Horned Red Grain, Lincoln.
3. Brittany.
4. April.
5. Arthur's Jersey (hardy, and productive on poor soils).
6. Black-jointed. 1841. — 27lbs. flour produced 37lbs. of good bread.
7. Old White-hair Welsh.
8. Red-hair Welsh.

9. Rivetts.
10. Coetbo, Brittany, elongated.
11. Coetbo, Brittany, compact.
12. Spanish.
13. Victoria, Caraccas.
14. Kubanka.
15. Cape of Good Hope.
16. Italian Red.
17. Kiel, Baltic.
18. Italy.
19. Egyptian.

TOTAL, 104 SPECIMENS.

Comparison and result:—

THE KENTISH OR JERSEY DOWNY, 1847.

One Quarter or 463¾ lbs. wheat produced 351¾ lbs. flour.

Do.   351¾ lbs. flour   do.   482 lbs. 8 oz. bread.

BALTIC OR ROSTOCK.

Do.   454 lbs. wheat produced 312 lbs. flour.
Do.   312 lbs. flour   do   398 lbs. 8 oz. bread.

From   482 lbs. 8 oz. Downy

Deduct 398 lbs. 8 oz. Rostock,

or 84 lbs. excess over the Rostock on one quarter, or excess over one acre at 6 qrs. to the acre, 504 lbs. of bread, the supply of one person for a year; the excess over some more inferior varieties, as to quantity of produce and yield of flour, being far greater.

DISTINCTIONS
OBTAINED BY THE WRITER AFTER THE APPEARANCE OF THE FIRST EDITION.

MEMBRE HONORAIRE DE LA SOCIÉTÉ D'AGRICULTURE DE L'ARRONDISSEMENT D'AVRANCHES, FRANCE, 1838.

DIPLOME DE MEMBRE CORRESPONDANT DE LA SOCIÉTÉ NANTAISE D'HORTICULTURE, FRANCE, 1838.

MEMBER OF THE SOCIETY OF ARTS, 1838.

MÉDAILLE D'HONNEUR ACADEMIE DE L'INDUSTRIE AGRICOLE, MANUFACTURIÈRE ET COMMERCIALE, PARIS, 1838.

DIPLOME DE MEMBRE TITULAIRE SOCIÉTÉ FRANÇAISE DE STATISQUE UNIVERSELLE, 1838.

DIPLOME DE VICE-PRESIDENT DE L'INSTITUT D'AFRIQUE À PARIS, 1840.

SILVER MEDAL OF THE HIGHLAND AND AGRICULTURAL SOCIETY OF SCOTLAND, 1840.

FELLOW OF THE ROYAL SOCIETY, 1843.

HONORARY MEMBER OF THE PHILADELPHIA SOCIETY FOR PROMOTING AGRICULTURE, UNITED STATES OF AMERICA, 1844.

HONORARY AND CORRESPONDING MEMBER OF THE NEW YORK STATE AGRICULTURAL SOCIETY, U.S.N.A., 1850.

PRIZE MEDAL, GRAND BRONZE, CLASS 3, INTERNATIONAL EXHIBITION, 1851.

DEDICATION.

TO THE

ROYAL AGRICULTURAL SOCIETY OF ENGLAND.

GENTLEMEN,

Having had the honour and great gratification of assisting in the formation of the Central Agricultural Society of Great Britain and Ireland, I now do myself the honour to dedicate this, my Second Edition on the VARIETIES AND PROPERTIES OF WHEAT, after thirty-five years of experimental research on this most important food of man, to the Royal Agricultural Society of England, which I affirm has conferred a more enduring benefit on the farming interest of this nation than any former association. Having also witnessed with admiration so many individuals of various rank and political opinions setting them aside to unite for the common interests of Agriculture, I consider it becomes us all to work for the common good, and endeavour to assist the farmer, in keeping alive and continuing those researches which have already so greatly improved the agriculture of the country.

Many of you, no doubt, have inspected the collection of one hundred and four varieties of wheat which I exhibited at the Great International Exhibition of 1851.* To these have been added, by the intelligent care of farmers, very many more.

That among these varieties, there are some that will thrive better than others, in the particular soils and situations adapted to each, all over the kingdom, is my firm belief. Thus, one ear of a superior variety, sowed grain by grain, and suffered to tiller apart, produced four pounds four ounces of wheat, whereas another ear, of an inferior sort, treated in the same manner, produced only one pound ten ounces,—is a proof that it is of paramount importance to select the most productive and farinaceous sorts of seed; it being obvious that a farmer who would have sown his whole crop with the last-named variety, would have probably been ruined, whereas the superior variety would have enabled him to farm with profit.

It is to the consideration of this general proposition that I continue to invite your attention, not to view it as a specimen of literary labour, with the eye of criticism, but as the statement of one who hopes he may not have laboured in vain for the

---

* For which the Author received the Grand Bronze Medal. That collection is now in the Kensington Museum.

interest of those whom he considers the true sinews of the land—its farmers. It is hoped it may lead to more extended and improved researches, in every county and province of the empire, as its principle extends to every cultivator of wheat throughout the universe. It is with extreme gratification that I have had to notice that in Great Britain, in France, and in America Agricultural Societies have been formed, and have given deep consideration and persistent encouragement to this special branch of husbandry.

The writer had the honour to receive the following encouragement from the venerable and much-to-be-regretted Father of Modern Agriculture, the Right Honourable Sir John Sinclair, on exposing his views to him :—

(1836.)

"My Dear Sir,—I had the pleasure of receiving your obliging communication from Belle Vue. It contains much important information. The plan you describe seems to be judiciously formed. I should be very glad, therefore, to see such an excellent system established also in this country; but ever since the extinction of the Board of Agriculture, which cost me so much trouble to establish and so much exertion to carry on, I have lost all hopes of seeing agriculture again placed in that splendid and flourishing state which it then exhibited.

"I hope, however, that this will not discourage you from continuing your exertions, the success of which I trust you will have the goodness, from time to time, occasionally to communicate to me.

"With my best wishes for your success in the important pursuits with which you are so laudably occupied,

"I remain, dear Sir,
"Very faithfully yours,
(Signed) "JOHN SINCLAIR.
"To Colonel Le Couteur, &c. &c. &c."

With this encouragement from my late friend, a philosopher of the most benevolent mind and extended knowledge, who had proved himself the farmer's friend and guide, I determine to submit my work to your favourable consideration, beseeching you to make allowances for the production of an unlettered soldier, who has for the last forty years turned his "sword into a ploughshare," but who courts the deepest inquiry into a most important subject.

  I have the honour to be,

      Gentlemen,

    Your very faithful and obedient Servant,

       J. LE COUTEUR.

Belle Vue, Jersey,
 January, 1872.

INTRODUCTION.

WHEN the Author first took up this subject of improving the growth of wheat, he was wholly unknown to agriculturists. He may now be pardoned for speaking with the authority of long and more recent experience.

In his First Edition he pointed out to farmers that the proper culture of wheat was then in a manner unknown, or unpractised. Since, great and important advances have been made by farmers in all parts of the kingdom, both in the preparation of the soil and the selection of seed. Some thirty-six years ago, Professor La Gasca, Curator of the Royal Gardens at Madrid, whose extensive collections of the varieties of wheat, and botanical researches into its nature as a plant, chiefly scientific and theoretical, first led the Author to make practical experiments on the growth and properties of wheat as a nutriment, which have since led to important results.

At the period above-named, I accidentally saw, with astonishment and pleasure, about eighty distinct sorts of wheat growing in a nursery-garden in Jersey; some seven feet high, some only four; the ears of some three inches long, others six. Professor La Gasca, whose they were, happened to join me, and, though a stranger, he politely explained their nature to me.

I requested him to visit my crops the following day; I considered them as pure—at least, as unmixed—as those of my neighbours, when to my dismay, he drew from three fields three and twenty sorts—some white wheat, some red, some liver-coloured, some spring wheat; some dead ripe, the corn shaking out, some ripe, some half so, some in a milky state, and some green.

I reflected on the subject, and immediately became convinced that no crop in that state could either produce the greatest weight of corn, give the largest quantity of flour, or màke the best or lightest bread, such as would be produced from a field in an equal and perfect state of ripeness.

I directly conceived a plan to endeavour practically to ascertain the relative properties of the best and most productive sorts of wheat; I requested Professor La Gasca to show me those which he considered the best and most productive. He pointed out fourteen sorts: these I grew with extreme care, in the mode that will be described hereafter.

When the Professor saw the drift and result of my comparative experiments, he exclaimed, " Is it possible that in one twelvemonth you have *practically* obtained the knowledge of what I have been for five and twenty years studying *botanically*? But persevere; with diligence and courage, you will yet work out some great benefit for your country and for mankind."

It is to the prosecution of these researches, after a long period of years of close application, that I continue to call the attention of the agricultural world. The results to be obtained in agricultural experiments are necessarily slow; nearly a whole twelvemonth must elapse before the seed which has been put into the ground will be convertible into bread—the only valuable proof of the experiment. It is, therefore, by slow approaches that we shall arrive at the perfect knowledge of a result which, it is believed, will be most important in itself, and most valuable to all intelligent, industrious, and persevering farmers.

The great first principle I wish to advocate is the proper adaptation of varieties of wheat to the various soils and climates, since it is the suitableness of each sort to each soil that will enable the farmer to pay the rent of his land, by sowing one variety, whereas he would be unable to do so by attempting to grow another of a seemingly better sort.

If this end can be obtained, the object I have had

in view will be realized. The farmer will be placed in a better position than he otherwise would be; the productiveness of the soil will be enormously increased, inasmuch as many unproductive lands may be made to grow wheat suited to them, under a proper rotation of cropping and clean husbandry. This last I hold to be indispensable under all circumstances.

If I have been fortunate enough generally to convince agriculturists that I have advanced facts, and have carried conviction to their minds, the cultivation of the most farinaceous wheats—white, red, yellow, or liver-coloured—each suited to their peculiar soils, will become a science not unworthy the attention of the various Experimental Farms and Agricultural Colleges which have been established in Great Britain and elsewhere

THE PROPERTIES OF WHEAT.

CHAPTER I.

WHEAT—ITS ORIGIN AND VARIETIES.

It is not the intention to write an elaborate treatise on this subject, which, although interesting to the learned and scientific reader, would be of no practical utility to the farmer. It may, nevertheless, not be wholly uninteresting to look back a little into the history of Wheat.

We learn from the sacred volume that it was of the earliest culture—"*In the sweat of thy face shalt thou eat bread.*" It is, therefore, to be presumed that wheat was coeval with the Creation; and that, upwards of a thousand years before the Christian era, some improvement in its culture, and some knowledge of a superior variety, had been attained, by the circumstance of its being stated that "Judah traded in wheat of *Minnith;*" perhaps meaning that such wheat of Minnith was held to be in superior estimation. This may be the most ancient designation for any particular growth of wheat, the superiority of which at that early period had engaged public attention. Columella, who wrote about the time of our Lord, makes some interesting remarks on wheat. "The chief and the most profitable corns for men are common wheat and bearded wheat. We have known several kinds of wheat; but of these we must chiefly sow what is called the red wheat, because it excels both in weight and brightness.

"The white wheat must be placed in the second rank, of which the best sort in bread is deficient in weight.

"The *Trimestrian* shall be the third, which husbandmen are mighty glad to make use of; for when, by reason of great rains or any other cause, the early sowing has been omitted, they have recourse to this for their relief. It is a kind of white wheat. Pliny says that this is the most delicious and the daintiest of any sort of wheat, exceeding white, but without much substance or strength; only proper for moist tracts of land, such as those of Italy and some parts of Gaul; that it ripens equally, and that there is no sort of corn that suffers delay less, because it is so tender that such ears of it that are ripe presently shed their grains; but in the stalk it is in less danger than any other corn, for it holds its ear always upright, and does not contain the dews, which occasion blasting and mildew.

"The other sorts of wheat are altogether superfluous, unless any man has a mind to indulge a manifold variety and a vain-glorious fancy.

"But of bearded wheat we have commonly seen four sorts in use—namely, that which is called *Clusinian*, of a shining, bright, white colour; a bearded wheat, which is called *Venuculum*—one sort of it is of a fiery red colour, and another sort of it is white, but they are both heavier than the *Clusinian*; the *Trimestrian*, or that of three months' growth, which is called *Halicastrum*; and this is the chief, both for its weight and goodness. But these sorts, both of ordinary common wheat and of bearded wheat, must, for these reasons, be kept by husbandmen, because it rarely happens that any land is so situated that we can content ourselves with one sort of seed, some part of it happening, contrary to our expectation, to be wet or dry. But common wheat thrives best in a dry place, and bearded wheat is less affected by moisture."

Hence, it appears, the Romans were aware of the propriety of selecting their wheat; and that it was then believed that winter or beardless wheat was best suited to dry uplands, and bearded wheat to low or moist lands.

In addition to the winter wheats, some of which he states to be bearded, he distinctly alludes to *Trimestrian*, or spring wheat, of which I shall speak hereafter.

Since this article was written, a very interesting paper has appeared in the "Journal of the Royal Agricultural Society," Vol. XV. (1854), p. 167, "On the Species of *Œgilops* of the South of France, and their Transformation into Cultivated Wheat," by Mons. Esprit Fabre, of Ayde. Three kinds of *Œgilops* are frequently met with in the South of France and in other parts of the Mediterranean district. He also names a fourth. However, as the interest specially rests with the variety which becomes, under cultivation, a bearded wheat, I confine my extract to that variety; nevertheless, the whole article is worthy of perusal. Page 171 : "Cultivation of *Œgilops triticoides*, obtained from *Œ. ovata*—that is to say, yielded plants like *Triticum*. I was induced to cultivate *Œgilops triticoides*, derived from *ovata*, in the hope of obtaining cultivated wheat, or at least some analogous variety. The next chapter is an account of my experiments with this view. First year of cultivation, 1839. The plants were sown for the first time in 1838. In 1839 the flowering stems attained a height of from 70 to 80 centim. The plants ripened from the 15th to the 20th July. As a result I obtained five grains for one, and the grains were close, concave, and very hairy at the top. The ears were deciduous—that is to say, they broke and fell off as soon as ripe."

Monsieur Fabre goes on to describe twelve consecutive yearly sowings from 1838 up to 1850, when he concludes :—

"For twelve consecutive years I have thus cultivated *Œgilops triticoides*, and its products. I have seen them gradually attain perfection, and become at last a true wheat (*Triticum*) ; and I have never seen a single plant reassume its primitive form, that of *Œgilops Ovata L.* This form never reappeared." Finally he observes, "It is clear that a true *Triticum* was then obtained, for cultivation in the open fields for four successive years did not cause any change in its form, and it yielded produce similar to that of the other corn of the country." This very interesting article on the origin of that species of food of the greatest use to man will, it is believed, be very acceptable to Mr. Charles Darwin, should it meet his eye.

In Gerard's "Herbal," printed in London, 1660, only five kinds of wheat are enumerated, which are thus spoken of :—

"1. *Triticum Spicâ Muticâ*, white wheat. This kind of wheat, which Lobelius, distinguishing it by the eare, calleth *Spicâ Muticâ*, is the most principal of all other, whose eares are altogether bare and naked, without awnes or chaffie beards.

"2. The second kind of wheat, in root, stalkes,

joints, and blades, is like the precedent, differing onely in eare and number of graines, whereof this kinde doth abound, having an eare consisting of many ranks, which seemeth to make the eare double or square. The root and grain is like the other, but not bare and naked, but bristled or bearded, with many small and sharp eiles, or awnes, not unlike to those of barley.

"3. Flat wheat is like unto the other kindes of wheat in leaves, stalkes, and roots, but is bearded and bordered with rough and sharp eiles, wherein consists the difference. [I know not what our author means by flat wheat, but I conjecture it to be the long, rough-eared wheat, which hath blueish ears when it is ripe, in other things resembling the ordinary red wheat.]

"4. The fourth kinde is like the last described, and thus differeth from it, in that this kinde hath many eares coming forth of one great care, and the beards hereof be shorter than of the former kinde.

"5. Bright wheat is like the second before described, and differeth from it in that this kinde is four square, somewhat bright and shining, the other not.

"I think it a very fit thing [he states in a note] to adde in this place a rare observation, of the transmutation of one species into another, in plants; yet none that I have read have observed that two several graines, perfect in each respect, did grow at any time in one eare : the which I saw this yeare 1632, in an eare of white wheat, which was found by my very good friend Master John Goodyer, a man second to none in industrie and searching of plants, nor in his judgment or knowledge of them. This eare of wheat was as large and faire as most are, and about the middle thereof grew three or foure perfect oats[*] in all respects : which being hard to be found, I held very worthy of setting downe, for some reasons, not to be insisted upon in this place."

He also entertained the opinion that wheat, "*in a moist and darke soil, degenerateth sometime to be of another kinde.*"

The singular fact mentioned above relates to the chapter on the disposition of wheat to sport ; but I have copied it as I found it. I principally wished to show how few varieties were then known, and how indistinctly they were described.

Modern writers had merely designated a number of varieties, but no attempt had then been made to class them correctly, or to ascertain their relative values by comparison.

---

[*] In 1857 M. Jean Le Boutillier told me this day that about twenty years ago he saw the same thing—an ear of corn with two or three oats in it.

In Sinclair's "Hortus Gramineus Woburnensis," forty-two of the cultivated varieties are enumerated, as winter or spring wheats, according to the arrangement of Linnæus, which this illustrious writer has merely given as a sort of botanical classification. The *Maison Rustique*, for 1835, enumerates thirty-nine varieties; and although a short notice is given of them, it is by no means sufficient, as their farinaceous qualities are not explained, nor is the classification according to Professor La Gasca's notions, as he called all bearded wheats spring wheats; though he admitted many of them would be increased in produce by being sown as winter wheats, and that many winter wheats might be made as late, and produce as much as spring wheats.

It is a classification of wheat, pointing out the relative value of varieties—in their quantity of meal, the weight of bran and pollards, with the weight of straw of each, and their adaptation to soils—which is now required.

That this would be a desideratum, no one, I imagine, will deny; but that it requires time, attention, and perseverance to make such discoveries will also be conceded, when it is stated that I already possess upwards of one hundred and fifty varieties, or sub-varieties.

CHAPTER II.

FAULTS IN ORDINARY PRACTICE.

It may be useful first to point out the defects in the present practice of husbandry with respect to wheat. The usual mode, with the best farmers, is to purchase seed corn where it is supposed to be clean and pure; by the last expression meaning wheat of one sort, or as little mixed as possible. Thirty-five years ago, the ordinary practice with those who may be said to supply the nation was to procure seed wheat where it could be got cheapest, without regard to mixture or purity, provided the sample was good, and appeared likely to grow; others did worse, and imagined that poor, lean, shrivelled wheat, the refuse of their own stock, or some coming from a distance, as a change, was all that could be required to insure a crop. Other carelessness, previous to or after culture, need not here be treated of, as that would equally affect the best as well as the worst seed. One observation it would be well to make now, that the old practice of putting fresh manure to land intended for wheat is decidedly dangerous, inasmuch as it tends to produce much grass or straw, and less grain, which grain is also of a dark and coarse nature. Stable dung should be applied plentifully to the preparatory crop, and when lime or ashes are not procurable for the wheat crop, the early and free use of the hoe will supply their loss in a great measure ; but none save decomposed stable dung should be applied to wheat, if that manure be necessary. This is merely stated as a general observation, as there may be soils which, without manure, would be wholly unproductive ; the experience of the writer being at present chiefly limited to what are commonly held to be good soils.

The writer, in 1831, thought his crops were tolerably pure, yet, on Professor La Gasca walking through them, as he has stated in the Introduction, he selected from them twenty-three sorts, of which some have since been discovered, through the experimental researches made by the Author, to be three weeks later in ripening than others. Hence I repeat, it must be obvious that corn harvested in an unequal state of ripeness cannot be the best for the purpose of making bread, when the greater part of the grain has been reaped in the state the farmer considered was fittest for the miller ; whilst the lesser part has been either in a milky state, or much overripe, or some in states between both conditions, which it certainly could not be under such circumstances.

It must be obvious that the greatest quantity of farina or meal is not obtained from wheat reaped in this condition; the largest quantity would be obtained when every ear produced that fine, plump, thin-skinned, coffee-like looking grain which evidently contains much meal, in a delicate, transparent, thin-coated bran, such as some Dantzic, selected from the *high-mixed*, produces.

Hence it is assumed that to have the best bread from any variety of wheat, is to have it so pure, that, supposing it to be grown on a level space, with one exposition, it will all ripen at the same time; slight differences being allowed for variation of accidental subsoil, or soil, unequal distribution of manure or defective drainage; but, speaking generally, it will ripen equally. Such variety, therefore, having ripened alike, will probably, if grown on good Kentish, Essex, Devonshire, or other soils specially adapted to the growth of corn, be (if reaped at the proper moment) in that exact state of plump, round form which promises the greatest quantity of flour.

I must here observe, that the cause why so much wheat appears to have many shrivelled, lean, ill-grown grains in it, arises often from the unequal growth of the many varieties that lurk in the purest crop.

Much has been judiciously written on the growth and cultivation of wheat, which has tended to a material improvement in those farms where care has been taken, perceptible even to superficial observers. Until the Author had taken up this subject, no previous writer had yet called the attention of the agricultural world to the cultivation of pure sorts, originating from one single grain, or a single ear. It is contended that the want of this method had been the root of all the evil; many attempted to begin well, but few, if any, had thought of commencing from an original grain of acknowledged superiority, and persevering in keeping it pure.

This idea struck the Author so powerfully, on the first conversation he had with Professor La Gasca, that it has never quitted him. His project was considered visionary and unattainable. Old farmers said that as no farmer in the world had ever thought of separating and classing wheat, it could not be done; it was impossible to get a pure crop! The bees would mix the farina, mice would mix the grain, birds would do the same; if it had been feasible, it would have been tried before. Corn factors assured him that the climate of England was not calculated for the growth of such fine-skinned wheat as that of Dantzic, Volhynia, and Sandomir. Professor La Gasca alone perceived and approved of the Author's project.

The learned Professor had been theoretically employed in the classification and scientific examination of wheat as a botanical plant, in the research and consideration of all its varieties; but it had escaped him to consider it in its farinaceous properties with relation to the food of man. This last was the practical view the Author took of it, and he determined to attempt to discover which were the most productive varieties, by comparing their characters and produce, one with another.

CHAPTER III.

ON THE CHOICE OF SEED.

The usual mode with the generality of farmers is to procure any seed that any neighbour, enjoying the reputation of being a good farmer, may have to sell. A more intelligent class take care to procure their seed from a distance, to require that it is fine, perhaps even pure; they also have thought of changing or renewing their seed occasionally. A still more intelligent number having procured the best seed they could obtain of those sorts which observation and experience have led them to know as being best suited to their soil and climate, have further observed that mixtures in their crops prevented their ripening at the same moment, and have endeavoured to remedy this defect by making selections by hand of those varieties which appeared to them to be similar, and thus have greatly and manifestly improved their crop in produce and quality.

A few farmers have proceeded a step further, and from having observed a stray ear of apparently unusually prolific habits, have judiciously set it apart, and have raised a stock from it. Hence the Hedge Wheat, Hunters, Hicklings, and twenty more, that might be named ; but it is contended that it is not sufficient merely to have grown them pure for a short time ; it is necessary to keep them permanently so, if, after a comparative examination as to their relative produce in grain and meal, they shall be proved to be the best ; or otherwise to discard them for more valuable varieties.

This was the chief consideration which led me to make comparative experiments, in order to obtain the best seed.

Hence, as a first step towards improvement, Professor La Gasca having shown me four ears of those he considered the most productive, I sorted as many as I could collect, of precisely the same varieties, judging by their external appearance.

Such was my anxiety to attempt to raise a pure crop, that, in the month of November, I rubbed the corn from each ear of all the four sorts I had microscopically selected, throwing aside the damaged or ill-looking grains, and reserving only the plump and healthy.

The first selection was apparently one wholly of a Dantzic sort—white and smooth-eared. In the process of rubbing out the corn, I was much surprised to find that, though most of the grains were white, they differed greatly as to form ; some being round, some oval and peaked, some plump but very small, some more elongated, some with the skin or bran much thicker than others. There were also many with liver-coloured, yellow, and dark grains among the white.

The second sort was from a square, compact variety of wheat, the grains being very plump, round, of a coffee-like form, very thin-skinned and white. There was also a pale red inferior variety among it, much thicker-skinned, but without any perceptible external appearance in the ear.

The third was a downy or hoary variety, one of the "*Veloutés*" of the French, and "*Triticum Koëleri*" of Professor La Gasca; a velvety sort, which is supposed to be very permanent in its duration as relates to keeping pure. I found, moreover, that there were a few red grains, some yellow, and some liver-coloured sorts amongst this, in small proportions it is true, but being of prolific habits, subsequent experience has taught me that they would soon have destroyed the purity of the crop if cultivated without constant attention.

The fourth selection was from a variety of red ear with yellow grains, more peaked than the "*Golden Drop;*" these were all plump and well-grown, but though of productive habits, afford less flour and more bran than the white varieties. I discovered a red variety among it, bearing white grains, which I judged would be very prolific and hardy. I gave a sample of it to the Right Honourable Sir John Sinclair, who greatly encouraged me to prosecute my researches, as being of the highest importance. There were also red ears, bearing liver-coloured grains, but these were chiefly lean and ill-grown.

I generally, but not invariably, found that the grain of white corn was the plumpest, or possessing the greatest specific gravity, or largest quantity of meal—a subject to which I shall devote a short chapter.

The aspect of the grain in that dry season led me to suspect that white sorts of wheat will succeed best on dry soils and in warm climates, and that red and yellow, or the darker-coloured, prefer wet seasons or moist soils.

The care I took in making these selections, and the great number of sorts I found of all shades and colours, forming varieties and sub-varieties, as they are named by Professor La Gasca, confirmed my conviction that the only chance of having pure sorts was to raise them from single grains or single ears.

It is but fair to add that even the pains I took in making those first selections amply rewarded my labours, as the produce of my crops was increased from an average of about twenty-three or twenty-five bushels an acre to about thirty-four, and since I have raised wheat from single ears or carefully selected sorts, I have increased my crops to between forty and fifty bushels the acre. Hence, I have no doubt that, with extreme care in obtaining the best and most suitable sorts of wheat, the land in high tilth, with fine cultivation, may be made to produce sixty or seventy bushels the acre.

Columella, while recommending much attention to be paid in choosing seed, says: "I have this further direction to give, that when the corns are cut down, and brought into the threshing floor, we should even then think of making provision of seed for the future seed-time; for this is what Celsus says, 'Where the corn and crop is but small, we must pick out the best ears of corn, and of them lay up our seed separately by itself.'

"On the other hand, when we shall have a more plentiful harvest than ordinary, and a larger grain, whatever part of it we thresh out must be cleansed with the sieve; and that part of it which, because of its bulk and weight, subsides, and falls to the bottom of the sieve, must always be reserved for seed; for this is of very great advantage, because, unless such care be taken, corns degenerate, though more quickly indeed in moist places, as they also do in such as are dry. Nor is there yet any doubt but that from a strong seed there may be produced that which is not strong; but that which at first grew up small, it is manifest, can never receive strength, and grow large; therefore Virgil, as of other things, so of this particular concerning seeds, has reasoned excellently, and expressed himself in this manner :—

> " I've seen the largest seeds, tho' view'd with care,
> Degenerate, unless th' industrious hand
> Did yearly cull the largest. Thus all things,
> By fatal doom, grow worse, and, by degrees,
> Decay, forc'd back into their primevous state."

Thus, we perceive, the Romans, at the period of the Christian era, were urged to be careful in the selection of their seed wheat.

Mr. A. Hillyard, of Thorpelands, Northamptonshire, in the "Journal of the Royal Agricultural Society of England," Vol. III., 1842, p. 300, writes : " Mr. Sewell, of Bookham, Surrey, and Mr. Fisher Hobbs, Essex, whose white and brown wheats were selected for trial at Oxford in 1838, having each been kind enough to give me a bushel of their wheat, I had them dibbled in, with five other bushels of different kinds—namely, the Brown Lammas, grown at Burwell, Cambridgeshire; the Clover, a brown wheat; the Golden Drop; the Whittington, and my Snow-drop, white wheat—on seven measured half-acres, after mangold-wurzel. The result of this experiment strengthens the opinion

I have long entertained, that the brown Lammas
wheats, such as the Burwell and the Clover, are best
suited to loamy soils, and for general growth in *this*
county—besides which, in every market in the
county, it will always fetch a higher price than the
white. A greater quantity of wheat is *now produced
per acre* than formerly, by greater attention being
paid in selecting seed from the best and most prolific
kinds; and by close examination into growing crops,
many new and valuable varieties are likely to be
obtained, and thus there will be what is best suited
for every description of soil. The public are greatly
indebted to Colonel Le Couteur for giving the result of his experiments made as to the produce and
value of many varieties of wheat; but these experiments, carried on in the Island of Jersey, cannot be
satisfactorily conclusive for the Midland or Northern
counties of England." In the Prize Report of the
Agricultural Society of Shropshire, by Henry
Tanner, Vol. XIX., p. 36 : " *Wheat.*—This crop is
sometimes sown after a fallow; as on the heaviest
land. The month of October is the season for sowing. From two to two and a-half bushels of seed
are sown; the 'Old Red Wheat' being considered
the best variety. White wheats are generally objected to for autumn sowing, and whenever they
are sown it is in spring. In good seasons from

thirty-six to forty bushels are grown. Wheat usually follows the breaking up of the clover-ley." In the Prize Essay on the Farming of Buckinghamshire, by Mr. Clare Sewell Read, Vol. XVI., p. 290, we see that the clover-ley is usually ploughed but once for wheat, with some exceptions in heavy lands, which examine. The season for wheat-sowing is much later than it was in 1809; then, on the elevated part of the chalk hills, wheat was sown before the old crop was reaped. Now, in the up-hill country, they begin in September, and in other parts of the county the planting is extended to the middle of November. The south of the county is celebrated for producing some splendid samples of Chidham wheat (which we have admired), but, like all fine wheats, it is a shy yielder, and much of the Barwell, red, and similar wheats are grown instead. On the light lands of the other parts of Bucks, the Spalding and red Lammas are mostly grown, while on the clays the Hopetoun and Old Suffolk appear favourite white varieties. The yield of wheat on mixed loams and good clays is considered to average four quarters; on the cold wet clays, and on the Chiltern hills, three quarters per acre would be a fair crop. The average yield of wheat in the county in the last report was stated to be nearly twenty-five bushels. The Middlesex Prize Essay, by the Rev.

J. C. Clutterbuck, Vol. IV., Part I, p. 17: "We learn that at fourteen miles from Charing Cross, on a farm of six hundred acres, where the land is flat and well adapted for steam cultivation, which has here been introduced, and which succeeds well in dry weather, though, when wet, the land yields too readily to the pressure of the machine—the key to the rotation of crops is the growth of wheat every *three years*. Thus, as a rule, one-third of the farm is under wheat, one-third barley and oats, one-third beans, peas, clover, and roots. The favourite wheat here and on the best land in Middlesex is Chidham, varied with Golden Drop and others."

In South Staffordshire, Mr. E. Evershed, Vol. V., Part II, p. 293, 1869, reports that wheat is usually grown in a four-course rotation, that Talavera is usually sown in February. Mr. H. M. Jenkins reports on the Aylesby, Riby, and Rothwell Farms, near Grimsby, Lincolnshire, in the occupation of Mr. W. Torr, Vol. V., Part II, p. 423, 1869 : "*Wheat.—* Except on the strong land at Aylesby, the seeds are always ploughed and pressed early, and the land is left thus until the end of September or the beginning of October. The strong land seeds are generally broken up by the steam cultivator at a cost of about 12s. an acre, and the land is afterwards ploughed and pressed. Any portion which seemed to require it would have a dressing of summer-made fold-yard manure before ploughing; and another portion would probably be top-dressed with 2 cwt. of guano and 3 cwt. of salt, early in the spring. The seed, after having been dressed with arsenic, or preferably with blue vitriol, is drilled with an ordinary corn-drill, from eight pecks on the strong land to twelve on the wold land being used to the acre. Oxford Prize (a red wheat) is the kind usually sown."

Mr. H. M. Jenkins reports of "The Lodge Farm," Castle Acre, Norfolk, formerly in the occupation of the celebrated Mr. John Hudson, Vol. V., Part II., p. 466, 1869 : " *Wheat.*—The clover-ley is manured with ten loads of farm-yard manure as soon as possible after the cow-grass has been mown, or the trefoil, or White Dutch, have been fed off. The manuring is generally done in July, August, and September. The land is then ploughed to a depth of about five inches, heavily rolled, sometimes with a Cambridge roller, and harrowed *four* times, and afterwards drilled with from eight pecks of *Spalding* wheat, at the commencement of the season, to *ten* pecks at the end of the year, the drills being seven inches apart. In either February or March the wheat is hoed either by horse or by hand, and is top-dressed with 2 cwt. of guano per acre. Previous to sowing, the wheat is dressed with Down's Farmers' Friend. Near Salisbury, on the Bulbridge and Ugford Farm (wheat), immediately before the seeds are broken up, the land receives a dressing of fifteen two-horse loads of farm-yard manure per acre; but the land, after turnips, is not manured, having been manured for the wheat crop. From two and a half to three bushels of two-thirds Browick red wheat and one-third of a white sort, for early sowing in October; later sowing, with *Nursery* wheat, drilled in rows, eight inches apart, with a Suffolk drill. In spring the land is horse-hoed, the light chalky brows are top-dressed with a mixture of $1\frac{1}{2}$ cwt. guano, $\frac{1}{2}$ cwt. nitrate of soda, and 2 cwt. of salt."*

* In all cases where reference is made to a volume, it will apply to the "Journal' of the Royal Agricultural Society of England," unless specially stated.

CHAPTER IV.

A FIRST COMPARATIVE EXPERIMENT.

PERCEIVING that there were so many varieties of wheat of similar external appearance as even to baffle the experienced eye of Professor La Gasca, who once more obligingly pointed out several varieties of different colours which he suspected to be the most productive, I proceeded to put into practice what had occurred to me to be the only secure mode to insure the growth of pure sorts of wheat—namely, to grow them from single grains, or from single ears, and to follow up the plan, by afterwards sowing only the produce of the most productive, so as to form a selective stock.

Hence at the same time that I grew the sorts selected by the eye, in a field, drilled near other corn, in order to secure them from the birds, thus greatly improving the purity of my general crops, I adopted the following method to grow the most pure and farinaceous wheats.

The number of grains in the ears, of fourteen sorts, were carefully counted ; in the smallest ear there were twenty-three grains, in the largest seventy-four.

The soil intended for their reception was a fine rich loam, several feet in depth, over red clay; a bushel of ashes of sea-weed was spread over the surface, which was dug about the same depth that the plough was intended to turn the furrow, for a wheat crop. The seed having been soaked in strong brine, in separate glasses, was then dried with slacked lime; the drills were made nine inches apart, and the grains were dropped in singly, at about three inches depth, at distances from each other of from three inches to eleven; the whole being in a square of twenty-two feet, or a perch (Jersey).

By referring to the Table at page 59, it should be noticed that the rows Nos. 15 and 16, which were sown very thick, and rows 17, 18, and 19, which were sown moderately thick, about as much so as by a drill machine, at the rate of two or three bushels to the acre, appeared above ground on the 24th of December, or in seventeen days; whereas all the single grains, of every sort, came up *two days later*— a curious but satisfactory proof, which experiments repeated since for the purpose have confirmed, that the grains of wheat, when sown thickly, impart a certain degree of warmth to each other and to the soil which hastens their growth two or three days earlier than a single grain.

Owing either to the cold, worms, or birds (although

TABLE No. I.

REMARKS on an Experiment made on fourteen varieties of Wheat, sown on the 7th December, 1862. Each row contained the grains of a single ear of corn; they had been soaked in brine for an hour, then dried as usual with lime. 27 = 1 denotes that 27 grains are equal to 1 scruple, apothecaries' weight, &c.

Nos.	VARIETY AND DESCRIPTION.	Seeds sown.	Sample.	Up.	Died.	Ripe.	No. of Ears	Average of Tillers.	Grains in best Ear.	Height.	Weight of Corn.	Weight of Straw.	REMARKS.
1	Triticum (Dantzic) Hybridum Candidum	64	27 = 1	Dec 26	3	Aug. 5	625	10	70	ft. in. 4 8	lb. oz. gr. 3 3 2	lb. oz. 3 9	White straw, fine.
2	Trit. Hyb. Album Densum.—Round White	62	28 = 1	do.	7	do.	562	10	81	4 8	2 12 4	3 4	Stout straw.
3	Trit. Hyb. Album Densum.—Rubellum (reddish)	53	27 = 1	do.	2	do.	556	10	86	4 5	2 12 7	3 6	Do. Do.
4	Trit. Hyb. (No. 6 c.)—Fine White	50	24 = 1	do.	4	do.	662	14	72	4 5	3 1 11	3 6	Straw very strong and thick.
5	Trit. Hyb. Coturianum.— Seedling—Fine White	24	20 = 1	do.	0	do.	399	16	72	4 4	1 14 7½	2 4	Slight straw.
6	Trit. Koeleri, No. 1.—White Downy	44	22 = 1	do.	4	6th	627	15	58	4 7	3 3 2	3 12	Do. Do.
7	Trit. Koeleri Coturianum.—Seedling Red Downy	24	18 = 1	do.	1	do.	350	15	55	4 4	2 6 0	2 2	Do. Do.
8	Trit. Koeleri.—White Downy	65	23 = 1	do.	9	do.	649	11	68	4 4	4 9 0	3 13	Fine Do.
9	Trit. Hyb.—Red Compact—Plump Whitish	40	23 = 1	do.	5	8th	355	8	57	4 0	3 4 0	3 15	Coarse Do.
10	Trit. Hyb.—Red Ear—Whitish	74	27 = 1	do.	7	6th	508	7	74	4 6	3 8 6	1 9	Reddish Do.
11	Trit. Hyb.—White Ear—Reddish Yellow Grain	60	21 = 1	do.	3	2nd	461	8	62	4 9	3 2 4	2 . 9	Do. Do.
12	Trit. Hyb.—Yellow	74	25 = 1	do.	11	1st	578	9	78	5 6	2 10 3	3 12	Straw white and stout.
13	Trit. Hyd.—Grand Rubellum—Liver coloured	58	24 = 1	do.	14	5th	380	8	59	4 8	2 7 7	2 7	Coarse.
14	Trit. Hyb.—Reddish Yellow Grain	62	24 = 1	24th	4	do.	363	6	64	4 11	1 10 6	2 5	Fine white straw.
15	Sown thick from a Pint of Seed similar to No. 1, selected by Professor La Gasca.	thk.	...	do.	...	do.	...	...	...	5 6	3 6 5	6 10	Do. Do.
16		do. less	...	do.	...	do.	...	...	...	...	3 0 6	5 11¾	Do. Do.
17		do.	...	do.	...	do.	...	...	...	...	2 0 6	3 13	Do. Do.
18	White Dantzic	do.	...	do.	...	do.	...	...	...	...	2 11 2	4 12¼	Do. Do.
19		do.	...	do.	...	do.	...	...	...	...	3 3 0	6 10	Do. Do.

care was taken to watch the corn), or other unknown causes, several of the single grains never came up, as will be seen by Table 1. No. 1, How many died. No. 13, called by the Professor, *Grand Rubellum*, or the red Lammas wheat, out of 58 grains, lost 14 ; whereas No. 5, the *Coturianum*, lost none. No. 1, a variety suspected to be delicate, but which proved one of the best wheats, both for produce and meal, from 64 grains only lost 3. In this manner I was led to judge of the hardiness of the varieties, and I was well pleased to observe that the white, or most valuable sorts, were full as hardy as the red.

It appeared that out of seven hundred and fifty-four grains, the whole number sown singly, seventy-four never came up ; a loss of nearly one-tenth, even with the care and attention I bestowed on them.

I have further discovered that some sorts are still more delicate, and of very precarious and uncertain habits.

The habit of growth of many varieties differs very considerably ; some being of a close, upright nature, others spreading and trailing along the ground ; some tillering sooner than others; those in the experiment had all done so by the middle of March. On the 27th, they were hoed for the second and last time, and were afterwards perfectly free from weeds.

I was not, at that early period of my research, so

attentive to the moment of flowering as I could have wished. It would, however, have been my desire to have noted the period of flowering of the different varieties, but as any remarks on this head, founded on the mild climate of Jersey, would have failed as a guide to farmers in less genial climates, that branch of research has been omitted; otherwise the knowledge of that precise moment might prove of the greatest importance to all intelligent farmers, there being an interval of a week or ten days in the period of flowering of some of the sorts. Hence, judicious selection, with due care as to the time of sowing the variety that will soonest come into flower, would enable them not only to keep their crops from intercrossing by the intermixture of their pollen, but, as they ripen in succession, would enable them also to bring in their crops in rotation as each variety ripens, without being hurried by their whole crop being fit for harvesting at the same moment, which is now too often the case.

It may be noticed that a single grain, picked up by me on the high road by chance, which I immediately perceived to be of an entirely different form and of a larger size than any I had yet seen, though sown a week later than the others, was the first to ripen, and was cut on the 31st of July. It has still preserved its early habit, which I know, having now a small field of it.

No. 9, the latest, was only ripe on the 8th of August. This difference in the period of flowering and ripening could further be increased by arrangement as to exposition and soil.

The next and chief object of attention was their comparative produce in grain (see Table II.).

No. 1 produced 3 lbs. 3 oz. from 61 grains, and 3 lbs. 9 oz. weight of straw, of a beautiful white colour, whereas No. 14, a red variety, only produced from 59 grains 1 lb. 10 oz. of wheat and 2 lbs. 5 oz. of straw. Here, then, was an immense advantage in favour of No. 1, which produced nearly double the quantity of wheat and a third more straw, its average of tillers being ten, whereas that of the inferior sort was only six; and Professor La Gasca, it must be recollected, imagined that this last was one of the most productive varieties, evincing the positive necessity of comparative experiments to ascertain the relative produce of wheat, which the theory alone, even of the learned Professor himself, could never have discovered, he merely having judged, from the external appearance of the wheat, its squareness and compact form, than which nothing could have proved more deceptive.

No. 8, a downy variety, was still more productive than No. 1, as 55 grains produced 4 lbs. 4 oz. of wheat and 3 lbs. 13 oz. of straw, its average of tillers

TABLE No. II.

RETURN of Produce in Weight of Corn, taking an average from No. 7, which had just twenty-three grains sown, showing the relative weight of Produce, as well as the total weight of the 14 sorts.

Nos.	Grain grown.	Average.	Produced. lbs. oz. gros.	Relative Number.	Surplus.	Total.	Total Weight of Corn. lbs. oz. gros.
1	61	23 = 38 =	1 5 0 1 14 2	256	+ 366	= 625	3 3 2
2	55	23 = 82 =	1 4 4 1 8 0	253	+ 309	= 562	2 12 4
3	51	22 = 28 =	1 5 5 1 7 2	272	+ 284	= 556	2 12 7
4	46	23 = 23 =	1 9 11 1 8 0	350	+ 312	= 622	3 1 11
5	23	23 =	1 14 7½	387		= 387	1 14 7½
6	40	23 = 17 =	1 14 2 1 5 0	384	+ 243	= 627	3 3 2
7	23	23 =	1 9 6	350		= 350	1 9 6
8	56	23 = 33 =	1 13 0 2 7 0	262	+ 387	= 649	4 4 0
9	35	23 = 12 =	1 15 0 0 10 0	226	+ 129	= 355	2 9 0
10	67	23 = 44 =	0 15 0 2 9 0	182	+ 326	= 508	3 8 0
11	57	23 = 34 =	0 14 0 1 8 6	212	+ 249	= 461	2 4 6
12	63	23 = 40 =	1 0 3 1 10 0	226	+ 352	= 578	2 10 3
13	44	23 = 21 =	1 8 4 0 15 3	193	+ 187	= 380	2 7 7
14	59	23 = 36 =	0 10 7 0 15 1	147	× 216	= 363	1 10 0

680 Grains produced a Total Weight of 38 lbs. 7½ gros. from a little more than one ounce and a quarter of Corn.

being 11, the straw of a fine colour, and the sample very beautiful, though scarcely so fine or thin-skinned as No. 1. This produced nearly three times as much corn as No. 14, and a third more straw.

These comparisons decided me to attempt the future cultivation of those I had discovered to be the most productive by a comparison of the produce of a whole ear. From a further examination as to the relative produce of 23 grains of every sort, taking Nos. 5 and 7, which had but that number of grains in an ear, and by thus drawing two scales of comparison, I hoped that a satisfactory conclusion might be arrived at. Hence the minimum scale or number was fixed on to compare their relative produce from an equal number of grains. Thus No. 7, containing 23, the least number of grains in one ear, became the standard to compare the relative produce of the whole fourteen sorts.

By following up these comparisons, it was suspected that Nos. 5, 7, 3, and 1, were among the hardiest varieties; but here their merits in some degree cease, No. 8 being the most productive, and Nos. 1 and 6 being equal. No. 8 also is the second most productive in straw, the fourth in the average number of tillers, also the second in weight of grain, and the third in produce of flour. It was, therefore, believed to unite many good properties, and has proved to be a highly productive and valuable variety of a downy or hoary sort, with a roundish white grain, rather thin-skinned, producing very fine flour, which makes delicious white bread. It has produced fifty-one bushels to the acre. No. 1, being an ear of a fine variety of wheat from Dantzic, has also proved to be highly valuable, though the straw is so tall that it might be apt to lay in moist situations.

I was induced also to cultivate No. 5, being a seedling variety, not at all disposed to sport or change, producing a very fine round white sample : it has proved very productive. It produced from 23 grains more than any, but then it had the advantage of double distance between the grains, which doubtless tended to its increase. Its average of tillers was 16.

By an examination of the comparative list, at page 63, it will be perceived that it was easy to arrive at some sort of general conclusion by attention to the produce of ears that contained nearly the same number of grains, and again, by a second investigation as to their relative produce throughout the whole, to establish which were those most advisable for general crops.

The continued investigation of two subsequent years have further confirmed me in my original

F

opinions. I am now convinced that a proper selection of wheat is indispensable, my crops having almost doubled in produce since I have raised seed of a pure sort. Those intelligent and superior farmers who have already made great strides towards pure crops, by a careful selection of seed, whilst they may not reap so great an increase; yet to those, however, I hold out decided hopes of great improvement by the means I recommend.

It must appear obvious, from the tables I exhibit, that a farmer who would sow No. 14 on a soil which would equally suit No. 8 might be unable to pay his rent; whereas, had he happened to have sown No. 8, he would have had nearly three times more wheat, and a third more straw; hence, it must be clearly seen that in any intermixture of sorts in crops, some, as I have already stated, having no less than 23 varieties, the loss of produce, as compared with entirely pure crops, suited to the soil and climate, would be in exact proportion to the number of less productive sorts so intermixed.

CHAPTER V.

ON THE ROOTS AND GROWTH OF WHEAT.

IT has been stated that wheat, when sown in November or December, appears in seventeen or nineteen days. An excellent article in the "Georgical Essays" led me to repeat a course of experiments made by the author, who speaks of them in the following manner: "It is not sufficient for a farmer to be acquainted with the nature of different soils; he should also be acquainted with the nature of such plants as are used in field husbandry. The soil and roots are so intimately connected, that the knowledge of both becomes essential. Wheat has two sets of roots: the first comes immediately from the grain, the other shoots from the crown some time after. I shall distinguish them by *Seminal* and *Coronal* roots.

"Plants, according to their species, observe a regular uniformity in the manner of spreading their roots; for which reason the same grain cannot be continued long upon the same soil. Is it not that each takes from the earth such parts as are congenial? The food of all plants is the same; only some require more, some less; some take it near the surface, others seek it deeper. This opens to our view a noble field of instruction. A careful inspection of a healthy root will at once demonstrate the bias of nature. An examination of the soil will show how far that and the roots will coincide.

"This is the rational basis of the change of species so well understood in Norfolk, where tap-rooted plants always follow those that root superficially.

"Wheat being subject to the severity of winter, its roots are wonderfully disposed to withstand the inclemency of the season. A view of their shape will direct us in the manner of sowing that grain to the most advantage, and at the same time enable us to account for some of the phenomena observable in the growth of it. I have observed that wheat has a double root. The first, or *seminal* root, is pushed out at the same time with the germ, which, together with the farina, nourishes the plant until it has formed its crown."

As I think I have followed the same course of experiments with even more care than the author of the above extract, I shall state my own observations in corroboration of it.

PLATE I., FIG. 1.—Appearance of a grain of wheat which had been sown three inches deep, on the 12th

Plate I.

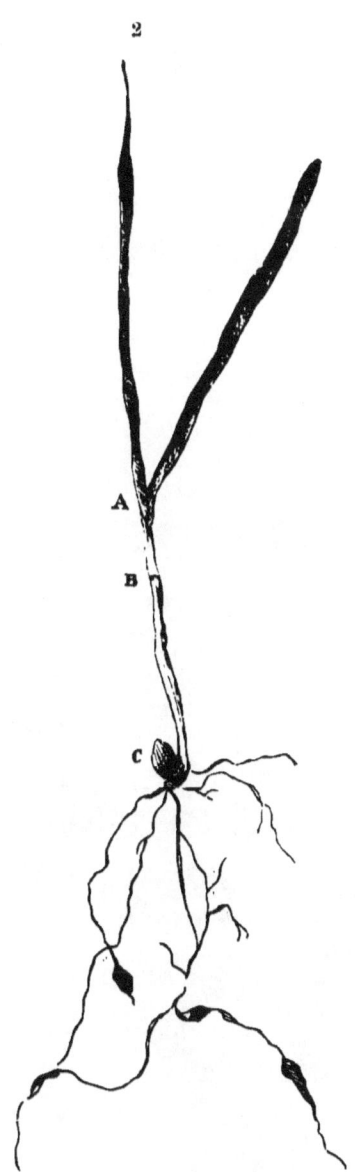

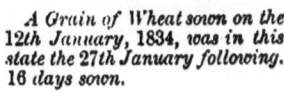

A Grain of Dantzic Wheat sown on the 7th December, 1832, and taken up on the 1st February following, had not yet formed its Coronal Roots.

A Grain of Wheat sown on the 12th January, 1834, was in this state the 27th January following. 16 days sown.

J. LE COUTEUR (after Nature).

Plate II.

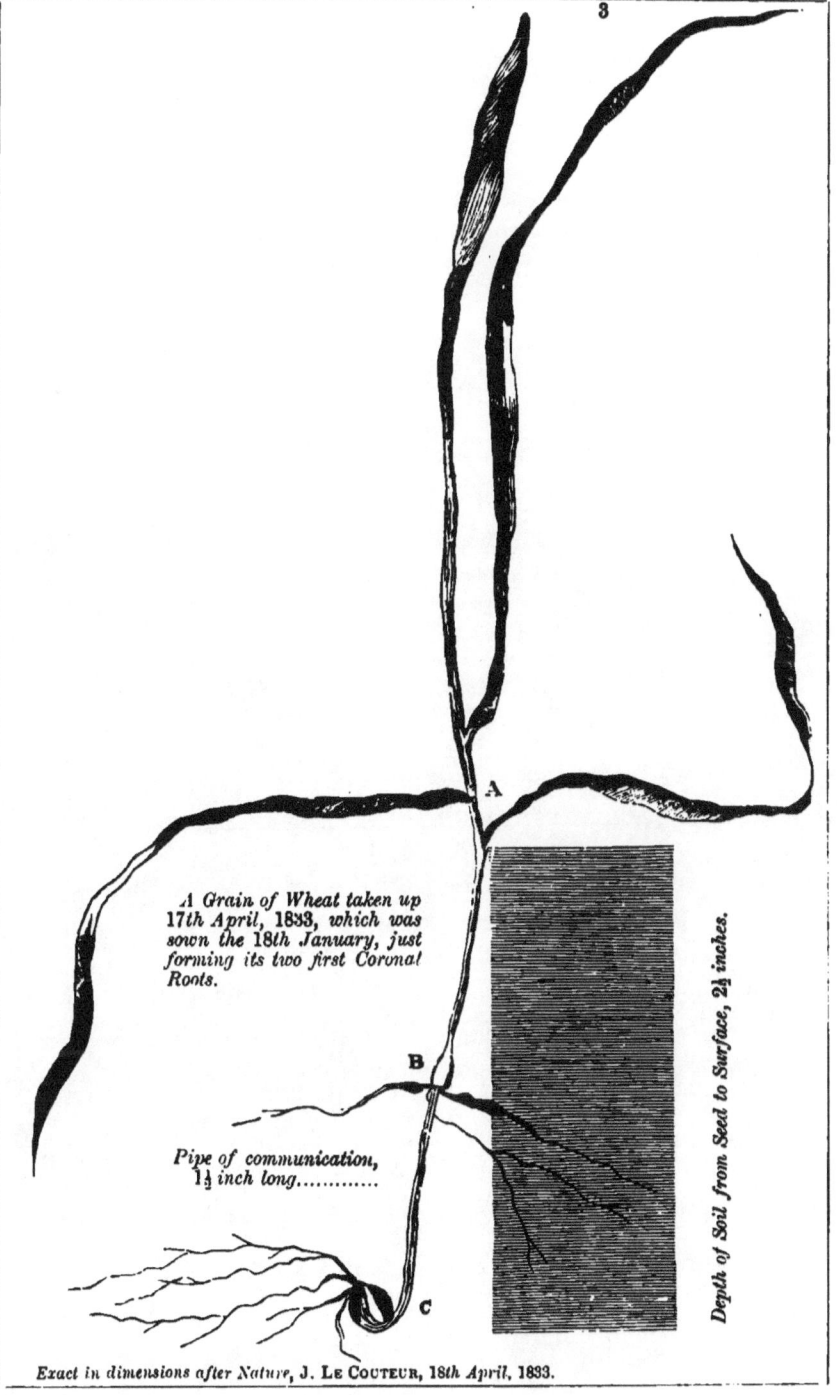

A Grain of Wheat taken up 17th April, 1833, which was sown the 18th January, just forming its two first Coronal Roots.

Pipe of communication, 1½ inch long............

Depth of Soil from Seed to Surface, 2½ inches.

Exact in dimensions after Nature, J. Le Couteur, 18th April, 1833.

January, after sixteen days' growth, with its germ and seminal root.

PLATE I., FIG. 2.—Appearance of a grain of wheat after fifty-two days' growth, the coronal roots not yet having pushed ; *a.* the origin of the crown from which the plant tillers ; *b.* the pipe of communication, covered with a membranous sheath ; *c.* the grain with its seminal roots.

PLATE II., FIG. 3.—A grain of wheat after sixty days' growth, just forming its upper set, or coronal roots. This was sown about three inches deep ; thus, the plants having been drawn from nature, and being exact in dimensions, show its process ; *a.* the crown of the plant beginning to tiller ; *b.* two coronal roots, an inch below the surface ; *c.* pipe of communication to the seed, one inch and a-half long.

The same author says: "In the spring, when the crown has become sufficiently large, it detaches a number of strong fibres, which push themselves obliquely downwards. These are the *coronal* roots. A small pipe preserves the communication between them and the *seminal* roots. It makes an essential part of the plant, and is observed to be longer or shorter, according to the depth that the seed has been buried. It is remarkable, however, that the crown is always formed just within the surface. Its place is the same, whether the grain has been sown deep or superficial. I believe I do not err when I call this *vegetable instinct*.

"As the increase and fructification of the plant depends upon the vigorous absorption of the coronal roots, it is no wonder that they should fix themselves so near the surface, where the soil is always the richest.

"From an attention to this circumstance, we are led to explain the operation of *top dressings*. In the northern counties, wheat is generally sown late. When the frost comes, the *coronal* roots, being young, are frequently chilled. This inconvenience may, however, be easily prevented, by sowing more early and burying the seed deeper. The *seminal* roots, being out of the reach of the frost, will then be enabled to send up nourishment to the crown, by means of the pipe of communication."

PLATE I., FIG. 4, shows a plant of wheat sown superficial; *a*. the crown and roots; *b*. the pipe of communication; *c*. the *seminal* roots, and capsule of the grain.

"Hence, it is obvious that wheat, sown superficially, must be exposed to the severity of the frost, from the shortness of the pipe of communication.

"The plant in that situation has no benefit from its double root. On the contrary, when the grain has been properly covered, the *seminal* and *coronal* roots are kept at a reasonable distance. The crown being well nourished during the winter, sends up numerous stalks in the spring. On the tillering of the corn the goodness of the crop *principally depends.*

" A field of wheat, dibbled, or sown in equi-distant rows by the drill plough, always makes a better appearance than one sown with the harrow. In the one the pipe of communication is regularly of the same length; but in the other it is irregular, being either too long or too short."

The able writer whom I have thus largely quoted, says, truly, that a noble field of instruction is here opened to our view; the double set of roots, thrown out by wheat, showing clearly that the first set, formed from the seed itself, and shooting downwards, seek their nourishment and freshness from below; while the upper set, or coronal roots, receive theirs from the richer particles of the manure which rise near the surface of the soil, also from top dressings, and from the influences of the atmosphere.

This theory appeared so plausible and consonant to common sense, that the Author, a few years back, was induced to plough in some fine seed of Dantzic wheat, about seven or eight inches deep.

It had been soaked, pickled, and limed, and was in a rather pulpy, soft state; the consequence was that, being buried *too deep*, and the winter and spring proving cold and wet, a vast quantity of the seed rotted instead of germinating, and proved a very losing crop, much to his regret and mortification. Thus it is of the utmost importance to avoid running into extremes in the prosecution of any new experiment, how plausible soever it may appear. Had the seed been sown at four inches depth, it probably would have all germinated, or even had it been less soaked, and pickled a less time, it would have reached maturity. But the intention was to have the seminal roots at as great a distance from the coronal roots as possible, in order that their nourishment should be drawn from opposite sources and in larger quantities.

The medium distance has ever since been followed —from three to four inches—which appears to answer perfectly in the climate of England as well as that of Jersey.

It may be well to notice that nature has in some measure pointed out that wheat may be sown quite superficial, as self-sown wheat is frequently seen very rich and fine, under which circumstances it may not have been buried a quarter of an inch, even supposing the wind and rain to have favoured its deposition.

Hence, it may be argued that wheat does not require to be sown very deep, but that a medium depth, sufficient to protect it from frost, so as also to enable its distinct set of roots to seek their food in different channels, is the safest practice ; the exact depth being a question of local experience, in relation with the nature of the soil and climate.

The extraordinary and valuable propensity of some varieties of wheat to tiller, while others will by no means do so much, is connected with this chapter.

One plant, from a single grain, of a downy variety, in 1862 threw out 32 tillers ; all produced ears, with an average of 50 grains to each, or 1,600 grains from one—an enormous produce, which no field cultivation could be fairly expected to attain, as it is not the extraordinary quantities which art may produce, either by extreme care, sub-division, and transplantation, that should be brought under the consideration of farmers ; but the fair and legitimate mode of husbandry, attainable to all who will devote to its pursuit that industry and inquiry without which their art is a mere mechanical operation, throwing in a little seed and leaving nature to do the rest. The average tillering on that productive variety I have alluded to was *fifteen* on forty plants, clearly evincing a prolific habit which has since been established. To ascertain this fertile habit was one of the great objects I had in view.

A very important paper, "On the Roots of the

Wheat Plant," by James Brickman, Professor of Geology and Botany in the Royal Agricultural College (a prize essay), is to be seen in Vol. XVII., page 172. The learned Professor has gone scientifically into the process of growth of the wheat from its seed, with a careful explanation of its development. Although the general mode of culture therein advocated essentially agrees with the experiments, it is stated (page 177) : " This table demonstrates what I have found in my own experiments in wheat planting—that from one to two inches is the best depth ; beyond this the plant becomes liable to joint-rooting, and, besides losing much time in coming up, they become thin and attenuated, and do not *stool* or *tiller* ; or if so, this process is weak and irregular." As reference is next made to the diagram $2aa$, I refer the reader to page 176, where the diagram is to be seen with the whole essay, which is of high interest. Although the depth which I have advocated —three inches—does not differ essentially from the one and the two inches recommended by the learned Professor, I submit, for the careful consideration of the practical farmer, whether in stiff soils a depth of one or two inches may not be fittest, whereas in light, friable soils, a depth of three inches may not be securest, so as to enable the seminal and coronal roots to take a firm grip of the soil. I had adverted to the practice insisted on by the Professor. In choosing wheat for seed, attention should always be paid to the circumstances of climate and soil; seed wheat should always be chosen from a poorer soil, for growth on a richer one; and from a cold climate for cultivation in a warmer. Acting contrary to this rule often induces disease and shortness in the yield.

CHAPTER VI.

ON THE NECESSITY OF PRESERVING CROPS PURE.

Some corn factors have declared that it will be impossible to grow wheat in this country of such fineness, whiteness, and beauty as is raised in the Polish provinces of Volhynia and Sandomir. Unquestionably, if success should attend the British husbandmen in discovering a variety as plump, white, and thin-skinned as the celebrated white sort, a small portion of which forms the precious part of that which is imported under the name of "high mixed," it might prove an interference with their line of business, as the English baker would then look to the English farmer for the most valuable meal he requires.

In almost every branch of Horticulture or Floriculture, Science, to meet the calls of luxury, has succeeded in triumphing over the impediments opposed to it by climate and distance. The pine, the peach, and melon are grown in equal—nay, some assert in greater—perfection in England than the indigenous fruit; and the dahlia, geranium, and lily tribes are more varied than in their native soils, and by seedlings are naturalized to ours.

These fruits and flowers are all classed and named; so are apples, pears, gooseberries, and a multitude of other fruits. The "Coccagee," or "Siberian bitter sweet," may be recommended as the best for cider, and no good ciderist would think of mixing every apple of every colour, ripe and unripe, for his mill, but makes his selections from pure sorts, whose properties and qualities are known. Strange that the same attention to selection and purity has been overlooked in that product which is the chief sustenance and comfort of the human race!

It only remains to discover those wheats which will grow in this climate without becoming flinty or thick-skinned; and if they cannot be obtained of varieties from abroad, they may be got from seedlings at home.

The Gracious Author of all things may have bounteously spread and multiplied this precious plant for the very purpose of leading men to seek out and discover those sorts which are adapted for their respective climates, and patient research only may be required to insure success. May not some intelligent husbandman in Volhynia, perhaps only a shrewd practical farmer, have discovered one sort which exactly suits its climate, as also the market it is intended for; and, without having written a treatise on the subject, may he not have distributed it as a precious boon to his countrymen? Is any corn factor prepared to say that all the wheat grown in Volhynia and Sandomir is plump and perfect—that no varieties are grown there which may appear coarse, lean, or shrivelled? Not having been there, I am unable to speak from personal experience, but evidence, as far as examination goes, and hearsay, lead one to believe that there, as well as elsewhere, seasons affect wheat and deteriorate it, both in its appearance and intrinsic value.

Hence it is confidently assumed that it only remains to be ascertained which are the best British wheats, in order to secure them of British growth from the climates of England, Ireland, and Scotland, as pure, plump, and thin-skinned as the choicest "high mixed."

I have shown the great productiveness of some sorts. I have often found among some of the Dantzic white wheat a coarse, red, thick-skinned sort, which in the ear was precisely similar in appearance to the proper one to be cultivated, even so similar as to be undistinguishable from it when viewed by Professor La Gasca and myself through a magnifying-glass; it was only on examining the grain that the inferiority of one of the two was perceivable. Therefore, where seed is not originally procured pure, it should be selected, and all the grains of a different shade from the approved sort removed, or the mixture and deterioration of a crop might be such as to lead a farmer to wonder how it could thus have *degenerated*, as it is termed, in the short space of a season or two, in defiance of the expense he may have incurred, or of his care and diligence.

Two years ago a farmer requested me to view a very *pure crop;* there was no mixture in it. In merely walking round the crop, which, in fact, was both pure and fine in common parlance, I selected from it ten varieties. Had I gone into it, ten more would probably have been found. A crop of this variety, the *Duck's Bill*, then originally procured from Kiel, in the Baltic, which I saw this year as a second vear's produce, is so intermixed as almost to make it difficult to pronounce what variety it is intended for.

The *Duck's Bill* to which I allude is very subject to shake out from the ear if at all over-ripe, and has proved to be only fit for making pastry, as it is too tenacious for the purpose of making household bread; hence the necessity of not only having wheat crops pure, but of knowing their particular qualities and farinaceous properties.

The Report on the Farm-prize Competition, 1870, Vol. VI., page 253, by Mr. Keary, gives an account of the Prize Farm held by Mrs. M. E. Millington, to which the judges awarded the One Hundred Guinea Cup, patriotically offered by Mr. Mason, of Eyrsham Hall, near Witney. This admirable lady, the winner over twenty-one competing farms, shows how the fair sex may excel even in the rougher trials of life when wet and wintry weather sometimes scares a sturdy and good farmer. This farm of 890 acres, called the "Ash Grove," is about fourteen miles from Oxford. It is worked on the four-course rotation system. The annual amount of Mrs. Millington's bill (1,200*l*.) was the great secret of her success, as I only speak of wheat. The treatment of the seed-shift, already described, which young farmers should consult, is the first preparation for the wheat crop. The clover-ley is ploughed up as soon as the weather permits, then rolled with the Cambridge roller, and about ten pecks of seed are drilled in during the month of October. The usual varieties sown are the Scotch white, Chaff red, and the improved Lincolnshire white. In the spring the wheat is hoed where it is thought necessary, but not otherwise. Somewhat later, thistles, docks, and weeds of all sorts are carefully taken out. No kind of top-dressing is applied to the wheat crop. The second Prize Farm of Mr. Treadwell, of Upper Winchenden, near Aylesbury, Bucks, to which the judges awarded the second prize of Fifty Pounds, given by the

Royal Agricultural Society, is farmed on a six-course system, almost to be described as a four-course rotation extended. The crops of wheat, barley, and oats, except a very few patches upon the thinnest soil, were remarkably clean, heavy, and good; plenty of straw, and large, well-filled ears. The wheats usually grown are *red Browick* and *Rivett*. None is sown till the beginning of November, when two bushels and one gallon per acre are drilled, and the quantity of seed is increased, as the season, advances to two bushels and three gallons. It is all hand-hoed twice in the spring, at a cost of 3s. 6d. per acre each time. It is cut with a fagging-hook, at an average cost of 11s. 0½d. to 12s. per acre, which includes tying and shocking (page 259). (Page 266) On the *commended* farms (Mr. N. Stilgoe's) wheat follows seeds. The land is ploughed in October, and pressed with a Cambridge roll. Sowing commences about the last week in October. Three bushels of seed are drilled per acre. *Burrett's red* and certain *white* varieties are the kinds most usually sown. In early spring the wheat is all hand-hoed, and later on thistles and weeds are carefully taken out. The wheat is cut by scythe, and is tied and shocked by the day; and the whole cost of wheat and barley harvest ranges from 12s. to 14s. per acre. Mr. Zachariah Stilgoe's farm at Atterbury, near

Banbury, is farmed much as that of Mr. N. Stilgoe's, and the *Burrett's red* and some white varieties are drilled on a stale furrow. On Captain Dashwood's farm at Kirklington the seeds are ploughed up early for wheat. No manure of any kind is applied in the autumn, but heavy top-dressing of nitrate of soda (as much as $1\frac{1}{2}$ cwt. per acre) is applied in the spring. *Talavera* and *Browick red*—a *mixture* of *white* and *red* wheats—are usually sown. From four to eight pecks of seed are drilled, ten inches apart, early in September. All the wheat is horse-hoed with Garrett's hoe early in the spring. It is generally cut by the fagging-hook, at a cost of 10s. per acre.

The foregoing description of the course of cropping adopted at Kirklington (which see) shows a very different system of farming from that pursued on the two prize farms, and I trust that Captain Dashwood will pardon me for making a comparison which may be instructive. The report says : "At Ash Grove and at Upper Winchendon, one-half only of the arable land is annually under white grain crops. The manure is all applied under-ground, and much reliance is placed upon the fertilizing power of cake and corn-eating sheep; but at Kirklington four-sixths of the arable land is given up to cereal crops, nitrate of soda being the great stimulant employed to force these extra crops from a somewhat exhausted soil. In very favourable seasons the system is said to answer, but this year it is certainly a failure. When we made our first inspection, in May, we were much struck with the general appearance of the farm; its large square fields, its clean cultivation, its straight drilling, and the business-like system of management which pervaded the whole concern. The young crops then looked green and flourishing, and we were not prepared to see so many acres of very light and inferior corn in the month of July. The whole blame is laid upon the season, but we think that want of condition is the real reason why light land at Kirklington has suffered so much more by drought than similar light land at Ardley. The fact is, that the system of growing corn by means of *stimulating manure* has been *pushed too far*, and the elements of fertility have *not been restored* to the soil in the same ratio as they have *been abstracted*. A trying season has come, and the crops have failed. I know that Mr. Lawes contends that corn may be grown year after year by the use of artificial manures. I doubt, however, whether upon light, thin soils the alternation of green and white crops can profitably be departed from. The inspection of the twenty-one competing farms has impressed me strongly with the opinion that it cannot." Lower down Mr. Keary says, "I believe that, in the long run, the true system is to endeavour to keep as much stock as possible, and not to grow corn upon too many acres. Stock must, and will, pay in this meat-consuming country; and the more stock a farmer keeps, the more he will have of that fertilizing matter wherewith to produce his cereal crops in the greatest perfection." Advice to which I earnestly call the attention of all young farmers.

CHAPTER VII.

ON MEAL AND BREAD.

THE main object of farmers has been merely to grow the largest possible crop of wheat, whereas the true aim of corn-growers should be, to produce the largest quantity of meal or flour. It is to the real nutriment we should look—to those transparent, thin-skinned wheats which are enveloped in so fine a husk or coat, or in so little bran, and contain so much meal, that, when compared with the coarse red wheats, one is almost surprised the plants should bear the same name; some of these last having a large portion of thick, coarse bran, with dark, coarse-looking flour, affording much less bread than the former varieties, and that of an inferior quality.

Some of these coarser descriptions of flour are prepared for sale by being mixed with potato flour, or other compounds, to make up that adulterated bread which is so often met with in cities. I have known bread, made from a judicious admixture of winter and spring wheats, to preserve a wholesome moisture, and to continue of good flavour for eight or ten days, and of brown bread for fourteen days;

whereas most London bread, thus kept, would have become so dry as to be scarcely eatable, perhaps even mouldy.

The difference of the nature and property of meal produced from various wheats is such, that it should be clearly made known and established, in order to enable millers to name the portion of dry light flour, or the portion of flour of a moist nature, required; or that the combination of two or more sorts would exactly suit their purpose.

The growers should supply the millers with wheat of known qualities, and the millers should then form the mixtures as the bakers might desire.

In the "Journal of the Royal Agricultural Society," Vol. IV., page 179 (Note, by Mr. John Hannam): "It is common to estimate the nutritious quality of flour or grain by its amount of gluten." Dr. Townes, in his Prize Essay on the Food of Plants, pages 545, 554 (*Ibid*), gives the proper mode for ascertaining the amount of gluten in meal or flour by careful analysis. At the time this work was written, I followed the method which had usually been had recourse to—namely, by washing the meal through a fine bag in a stream of water until no discolouration took place. By this mode, carried on during the space of one hour, I obtained the following result: A corn-meter, representing a weight of 64 lbs. of my Belle Vue Talavera wheat, grown at Belle Vue, on the 11th of December, 1861; on the 8th of September following, after being kept in a room at a temperature varying from 60 to 65 degrees (the high temperature being owing to the room being just over the kitchen stove), it had lost by desiccation 3 lbs., being 61 lbs. to the bushel. This being carefully ground in a hand mill, afforded 254 grains of gluten. Whereas a corn-meter full of the Belle Vue Talavera wheat, grown at Coul, in Scotland, by Sir George Mackenzie, weighed on same day (11th December, 1861) 65 lbs. to the bushel, and on the 8th of September, 1840, it weighed $62\frac{1}{2}$ lbs., having lost $2\frac{1}{2}$ lbs. by drying in the same room in which both samples were kept, and ground as above afforded 227 grains of gluten. Hence the sample grown in the warmer climate of Jersey yielded twenty-seven grains more gluten than the sample grown in the colder climate of Scotland.

It will be recollected that, in order to ascertain the relative specific gravity of each variety of corn, the number of grains were noted that exactly weighed a scruple. Such was their difference, that it only required fourteen grains of one sort, of my own growth, to weigh a scruple; whereas it took forty-two of a sample from the Baltic, which, probably, must have been kiln-dried, as not one grain sprouted. It is assumed that this may be a good mode of ascertaining which contains most meal, as it appears to be consonant to reason that the heaviest grains should generally contain the greatest portion of farina, though I am yet unprepared to say positively that the latter must be the finest or whitest.

This attempt to ascertain the comparative weight of many varieties, by merely weighing a scruple of each, led me to prosecute my researches from the straw and grain on to the meal itself, in order to be fully satisfied which of the fourteen sorts under experiment contained the greatest portion of meal or flour.

Hence I hoped to ascertain if the most productive sort in grain should also prove the most farinaceous —a great and important desideratum. I am truly happy to say that such was almost the result. I shall indicate how much further it requires to be prosecuted to establish it.

The mode I adopted was to strike a measure full of each sort of wheat, which was then ground by myself in a small mill. The scale of weights used was sixty-four grains (apothecaries' weight), equal to one gros, and eight gros equal to one ounce, of sixteen to the pound.

It will be seen, by referring to Table No. III.,

TABLE No. III.

RESULT of an Experiment to ascertain the Quality of Meal, or Flour and Bran, in each of the fourteen varieties under trial.

Nos.	DESCRIPTION OF GRAIN.	½ Gill Measure Weighed. oz. gros. grs.	Produced in Flour. oz. gros. grs.	Produced in Bran. oz. gros. grs.	Total in Grinding. oz. gros. grs.	Loss in Grinding. oz. gros. grs.
1	White Dantzic—large round	1 5 28	1 0 42	0 4 24	1 5 2	0 0 26
2	Small Round	1 4 50	0 7 50	0 4 34	1 4 24	0 0 30
3	Reddish Round	1 4 37	0 7 5	0 5 14	1 4 19	0 0 18
4	Fine White—longish	1 4 46	0 6 3	0 6 37	1 4 50	0 0 16
5	FineWhiteSeedling—roundish	1 4 39	0 6 3	0 6 20	1 4 32	0 0 7
6	Fine White	1 4 52	0 7 18	0 5 11	1 4 29	0 0 13
8	Coarse Yellow—round	1 4 50	0 6 51	0 5 41	1 4 28	0 0 22
7	Fine White	1 5 4	0 7 24	0 5 12	1 4 36	0 0 32
9	Plump Whitish—roundish	1 4 38	0 6 46	0 5 32	1 4 14	0 0 24
10	Whitish	1 4 39	0 7 20	0 5 4	1 4 24	0 0 15
11	Reddish Yellow	1 4 44	0 6 57	0 5 39	1 4 32	0 0 12
12	Yellow—round	1 4 44	0 6 8	0 6 26	1 4 34	0 0 10
13	Liver—elongated	1 4 32	0 6 34	0 5 44	1 4 14	0 0 18
14	Reddish Yellow—plump	1 4 28	0 6 28	0 5 29	1 3 57	0 0 31

that a measure of No. 1, or White Dantzic wheat, weighed one ounce, five gros, and twenty-eight grains; this produced one ounce and forty-two grains of flour, with only four gros and twenty-four grains of bran; whereas the most inferior variety, or that which produced most bran and least meal from the same measure, produced only six gros, three grains of flour, and six gros, thirty-seven grains of bran—in fact, more bran than flour. This, however, is not a conclusive experiment to determine the growth of wheat on an extensive scale, as no one, it is hoped, has yet had the misfortune to grow a pure crop of a very bad, unproductive sort. But, if such were the fact, the difference in the produce of meal, in addition to the excess in the produce of grain of the superior over the inferior variety, would, if carried over the five millions of acres employed in the cultivation of corn in the United Kingdom, make the quantity absolutely enormous.

Any person may, by examining the tables, find out the difference of produce in any two of the sorts, or the superiority of any one good sort over the other thirteen sorts, which together make up a mixture to be found in most fields, by which he may satisfy himself as to the positive advantage of establishing *which is the variety* of wheat best suited to his own particular locality.

The experiments made, as described above, have led to the results shown in the three following varieties of my own growth.

From a downy or hoary variety, eighteen pounds of flour, with half a pint of yeast, five quarts and a pint of water, and one ounce of salt, made *twenty-six pounds* of beautiful light white bread.

From a Dantzic wheat flour, the same quantity, with the same proportion of yeast, salt, and water, made *twenty-four pounds and a half* of very white bread, similar to French bread.

The same weight of spring wheat flour made *twenty-four* pounds of inferior brownish bread.

The same weight of Rostock and Dantzic flour from wheat grown in the Baltic made only *twenty-three* pounds of bread, very light and good, but not so white by many shades, or well flavoured, as that made from the two first varieties of home growth.

These experiments having been made in my own presence, may be relied on. The dough was worked in the French mode, not pushed down, turned and worked with closed hands, but drawn up into long strings and repeatedly lifted, in order to expose it to the action of the air as much as possible, which tends greatly to improve the bread by rendering it more light and easy of digestion.

The superiority of the meal of the hoary variety

of wheat, which furnished three pounds more bread on a baking of eighteen pounds of flour, or an increase of one-sixth over the Dantzic and Rostock, which was also a very fine sample of flour, is thus clearly established.

It is said in the article "Baking," in the second volume of the "Encyclopædia Britannica," "that a sack of flour weighing 280 lbs., and containing five bushels, is supposed capable of being baked into eighty loaves in the Act of Parliament regulating the assize upon bread. According to this estimate, one-fifth of the loaf consists of water and salt, the remaining four-fifths of flour. But the fact is that the number of quartern loaves that can be made from a sack of flour depends entirely upon the goodness of that article. Good flour will take more water than bad, and old flour than new. Sometimes, eighty-two, eighty-three, or even eighty-six loaves, may be made out of a sack; sometimes scarcely eighty."

Now, assuming these data to be correct, the results I have obtained prove that the hoary wheat, No. 8, will afford flour that will make ninety-three quartern loaves from a sack, being a superiority of ten loaves on each sack, taking the medium number, eighty-three; and this, be it observed, without adulteration, the pure home-made bread, unmixed with alum to whiten it, or potato meal to moisten it.

This superiority, be it further observed, is due to the good quality of the flour.

"HOW THE FRENCH OBTAIN FINE FLOUR.—In M. D'Arblay's establishments the harder kinds of wheat, chiefly Sardinian, Sicilian, and Russian, are ground; and by means of the adjusting process there applied, the grains are first ground high in the mill; the white middlings are then separated by coarse sieves and re-ground low in the mill; finally the flour is repeatedly passed through fine silk sieves. In the manufacture of these sieves the French excel; and the superior fineness of the French flour, so well adapted for patés and the like culinary preparations, in great measure depends upon the important part of the flour manufactory. By the combination of the superior sieves with the gruaux principle of grinding, the wheat flour may be made to contain more or less gluten in proportion to starch, and a saving of the finest and most nutritive portion of the flour is effected. There was no evidence in the British Department of the Paris Exposition of any improvement likely to render us less dependent upon France for the peculiarly fine kinds of flour which continue to be extensively imported for the purpose of mixing with and bettering our inferior flours. The gruaux principle of grinding is well worth the attention of the Australian colonists; the hard wheat of that climate most resembling those kinds of European wheat which M. D'Arblay finds best adapted for the application of his principle of flour grinding."—*Professor Owen's Report on Alimentary Substances in the Paris Exhibition.*

CHAPTER VIII.

ON MANURE FOR WHEAT.

THE effect of different manures on wheat is very remarkable. It will not be necessary to say much on the subject, as it is almost exhausted, having been fully treated by far abler pens; but having made some experiments on the subject, I may be excused for publishing their results.

I confine my observations to those manures which are within the reach of most farmers, with one or two exceptions.

Stable manure will, in ordinary good soils, have the effect of causing the plants to tiller much, or to make straw and grass, thereby diminishing the produce in grain and meal considerably.

Liquid manure, one-third stable drainings and two-thirds water, which I caused to be poured once over wheat that was just tillering, made the straw grow rank and coarse; the grain of every variety of wheat was dark and thick-skinned, hence containing less meal. The same quantity and mixture of liquid manure, poured a second time over another portion of wheat, caused it to grow so rank and full of leaves, rather than straw, that only a few of the plants produced ears of wheat, some having run up into sharp points, with merely the rudiments of ears indicated. The few ears that produced corn displayed it in its worst form, hardly in the shape of meal, of a doughy, soft texture, evidently unfit for the food of man; besides, some of them were smutty. Thus, an over-application of manure becomes a poison, precisely in the same manner, as in the human constitution, a surfeit is usually the parent of some disease.

The wheat, on either side of these experiments, which had only been manured with the ashes of Kelp, or Sea-weed, was healthy, productive, and farinaceous in the highest degree.

My attention was particularly called to the proper application of manures by an old and experienced farmer, who considered Kelp or the ashes of Rock Sea-weed—that which is cut—the best of all. I am convinced by subsequent experience that 2*l.* or 3*l.* worth of it per acre, spread at the proper period, about two months before sowing time, would always more than repay itself.

It attracts moisture from the atmosphere, it materially increases the volume of the grain and fineness of the sample; but does not add to the weight of the straw, though rendering it whiter and more nourishing to cattle. It causes the wheat to assume a rich healthy appearance, and is an excellent application, after a crop of potatoes or parsnips, both of which require land to be richly dressed with stable or other strong manures, and has not the effect of decomposing them, as lime does.

It is also destructive to insects, and to their eggs, which lie in the soil or turf; it forces the earthworms and wire-worms from their lurking places to come to the surface and die, particularly when laid on in a larger quantity than I have named; some farmers being in the habit of putting on double, even treble, the quantity above stated, but, I believe, without having produced proportionably larger crops from inferior land, though it has been asserted that its effect is very permanent, being especially apparent on the succeeding clover crops.

I am inclined to believe that paring and burning an old ley will almost produce an equally good effect, where the land is suited for it; for, although the ashes may not be of that superior quality, or possessing all those virtues peculiar to Kelp ashes, still the much greater portion of ashes that can by this means be spread on the land may make amends in quantity for quality.

An additional circumstance in favour of paring and burning is, that all the seeds of weeds, or the eggs of insects which lie concealed in the turf, are

H

thereby destroyed more effectually than by repeated ploughings.

The careful experience of thirty-five years on this head has convinced me of the propriety of this practice occasionally, especially on ground infested with couch or knot grass. From three acres of land that had been pared and burned, which produced five hundred and forty single-horse loads of ashes, I obtained a very heavy crop of turnips. The following year I raised ninety-one thousand pounds of potatoes; and, by an application of about forty-five bushels of lime per acre, I have since reaped fifty-one imperial bushels of beautiful wheat per acre; the straw, also, was of very fine growth, five feet high, and exceedingly white and bright.

Kelp ashes should lay on the surface of the soil a month or two previous to sowing time, in order to weaken their caustic power, or they are otherwise apt to burn the young and tender shoots of the corn, as well as the larvæ of insects; but, by laying a certain length of time on the surface, exposed to the action of the atmosphere, or perhaps, what would be better practice, merely lightly turned into the soil, they become eminently beneficial.

I am so partial to the use of vegetable ashes, that I should recommend those who have large woods or forests to employ women and children to collect the dry and broken boughs and under-shrubs, to be burned, for the sake of the ashes, which would be found nearly equal to those of sea-weed, and could thus be procured at a much cheaper rate, besides gaining the advantage of converting what is now wasted or neglected into a most valuable and permanent manure, perfectly free from weeds, and destructive to insects and worms.

Ashes are further beneficial, inasmuch as they attract the moisture from fogs and dews, and retain it a considerable length of time.

Lime is so well understood as a manure for wheat that it would be a mere waste of time to say more on the subject than as far as my own experience goes. It appears to impart a greater degree of whiteness to the straw than any other manure. Its other excellent qualities of absorbing moisture from the atmosphere in dry weather, on light or gravelly soils, and increasing the weight of the grain, are well understood. It is to be lamented that some general rule for its application is not made known, as, in the best books I have consulted on the subject, it varies in the extraordinary proportion of from fifty-six to five hundred bushels per acre, which last appears to me to be an absurd quantity.

I have found it to answer perfectly at the rate of forty to fifty bushels an acre on a good loam, and

I should apprehend that double that quantity ought to be sufficient for the poorest land ; unless it be to destroy moss, when a still larger top-dressing is required, which, if well harrowed in, does it effectually. This commixture of turf and lime, if soon after ploughed in, in turn becomes itself a manure for the very soil the turf previously rendered barren.

Soot is said to be an excellent top-dressing. I have tried it but once, without having perceived the advantageous results that are said to be derivable from it ; it is only in the environs of towns or villages that it can be obtained in sufficient quantity to be available to a large farmer.

Nitrate of soda is found in layers on the surface of the earth in the western part of South America, and is brought on mules to the coast, where it undergoes a process of refining, so that it never contains more than five per cent. of alloy in the original packages in the docks of London ; while saltpetre, or the nitrate of potash, has come over from the East Indies and Turkey, with from thirty to fifty per cent. of alloy.—(Note, p. 270, Vol. I., 1840.)

For full particulars of experiments made with manures, and references, see the articles in the "Journal of the Royal Agricultural Society." Nitrate of soda, 140 lbs. to the acre (David Barclay, Esq.)—result not conclusive (Part I., Vol. II., p. 118).

The singular variations in the results of many actual experiments with nitrate of soda by parties seeking to advance the cause of agricultural improvements, are calculated to discourage the use of it as a manure (p. 131). In Suffolk : "This year I have only used the nitrate of soda—1 cwt. per acre—first : For wheat on a fair light soil, sown on the 20th of May —the produce, 32 bushels per acre ; where no nitrate was sown, 27 bushels 2 pecks, being an excess of 4 bushels 2 pecks. Second : On better land, a fair loam, sown 26th of May, 1840 (both after clover)— produce, 36 bushels per acre ; without nitrate of soda, 30 bushels 2 pecks, being an excess of 5 bushels 2 pecks. In both cases one-sixth more of chaff and straw, but no improvement in the quality of the corn." Derbyshire—William Greaves, Bakewell : " I consider the nitrate of soda paid me very well." Gloucestershire—W. H. Hyatt, Esq., in an able article (p. 142) : "This result satisfactorily proves that the nitrate of soda used in the stone-brash, in good heart, produces an abundant wheat crop, though the risk of injury by weather from over luxuriance seems increased. Still, making every allowance for actual injury in this case, and for the outlay, the increased value of the produce gives an ample profit of 2l. 17s. 2d. an acre—a sum nearly double the rent of much of the adjacent land of similar quality." (P. 267, Vol. V., 1844) Experiments by John Hannam, from "Essay on Manures;" prize of 50*l*. from the Royal Highland Agricultural Society: Soil, thin limestone, worth 20s. per acre rental. Conclusions:—

1. Nitrate of soda, nitrate of potash and soot, have a tendency to increase the produce of wheat—both straw and grain.

2. That common salt has a slight tendency to increase the produce of grain, and to decrease the weight of straw (mark the *weight of straw*, as it will be observed—*vide* number of sheaves per rood—that it does not diminish the bulk), and that common salt increases the weight per bushel of the grain; thence it may, from these properties, be advantageously used as an auxiliary to other manures.

3. That sulphate of soda has *no* visible effects upon the wheat crop. The slight variation in yield of straw and grain may be fairly attributed to accidental circumstances, such as variation of soil, &c., as no two patches can be *perfectly* equal in every respect.

Mr. Lawes' report to the Earl of Leicester, on experiments conducted by Mr. Keary on the growth of wheat at Holkham Park Farm, Norfolk—(Vol. XVI., page 209)—is of great interest. Seven searching experiments were made. Nos. 1 to 7:—

No. 1. Always unmanured.
No. 2. Mineral manures alone.
No. 3. Ammonia salts alone; sown in the autumn.
No. 4. Ammonia salts alone; sown in the spring.
No. 5. Both the mineral manure and ammonia salts.
No. 6. Rape-cake.
No. 7. Farm-yard dung.

Those were carried on with diligent care, highly instructive to the scientific farmer—by whom I mean one given to research, as to the chemical natures of soils and their appropriate artificial manures. Nevertheless, I am aware that there exist a vast number of practical farmers who, by a close observance of the growth of their crops, become essentially scientific as regards their local soils and climates. A short notice of those experiments may be deemed of value. Full information can be obtained by reference to the reports. It is certain that no farmer of experience would persevere in trying to raise crops on unmanured land. Several artificial manures might not be obtainable, or, at least, at hand for experiments; hence, it would appear that the most simple might, as we see, be the most profitable for ordinary practice—for instance, as reported :—

	Offal.		Straw.
	B. P.	B. P.	Loads.
Rape-cake, at the rate of 2,000 lbs. to the acre, produced in the four years . .	147½ 0	2 2	8,240
A combination of *seven* muriates, sulphates, and superphosphates = 1,350 lbs. .	145½ 0	1 3½	8,515
Farm-yard dung, 14 tons . .	135 2	1 2	7,819

It would thus appear that the most simple mode of cultivating a good light soil produced the first and third best results—the combination of seven artificial manures being the second best of the seven. The relative cost of these manures would have been interesting to know, yet it is questionable whether such a mixture of manures could be found available for general practice. It would have been of much value to have known what would have been the effect of some cwt. of ammoniacal salts added to the stable dung. The report concludes : "What, then, is the lesson to practical farming which these experiments should teach us? It will not be supposed, because it is here shown that in a cultivated soil, of a comparatively light character, an increased growth of wheat may be obtained over a continuous series of years by the use of nitrogenous manures alone, that hence rotation and home-manuring should be abandoned, and that corn crops should be grown continuously by means of nitrogenous artificial manures. There cannot, however, be a doubt of the legitimacy of the inference from these and other experiments, that, *provided the land receive, in a course of years, a due share of the home manures derived from feeding of horses and other stock on the farm*, the mineral supplies of the soil will be amply sufficient to sustain an increased and even repeated growth of corn, by means of nitrogenous artificial manures, considerably beyond that which is recognized by the leases or the current practices of the day; and a further assurance that the necessary minerals are not likely to become deficient, under the *judicious* adoption of such an increased growth of corn, is to be found in the fact that there are few really large sources of nitrogenous manures which do not, at the same time, bring upon the land a considerable amount of some of the more important minerals also."

The lines relating to the use of *home manures* combined with nitrogenous artificial manures, have been understood, in the belief that such admixtures, inquiringly laid on the land, may be an admirable mode of investigation for permanent treatment. Professor Voelcker, in Vol. XVII., page 200, of his elaborately valuable Essay, gives an important hint to the practical farmer. It is particularly worthy of notice that the soluble ash of even *perfectly fresh dung* contains a very *high per-centage* of *phosphate of lime*, which I deem to be of essential value for the culture of wheat in some soils. At Vol. XXI., page 329, in the Prize Essay by Professor Tanner (page 331), we are told : " I have estimated, from the analyses given by Dr. Voelcker, as the results of an examination of farm-yard manure in its fresh and also in a well-rotted condition, that the ingredients in very superior manure, calculated at their market value, are worth 1s. per ton more when the dung is in a fresh condition than when it has become thoroughly decayed. When lime and dung are both to be used upon a fallow, care must be taken not to apply them at the same time; otherwise, from their combination on the surface, ammonia will be set free and lost in the atmosphere. But, with due precaution, the two may be employed in the same season, not only without loss, but with great advantage. The dung may generally be applied in a fresh state before the second spring ploughing, after which the lime may be spread on the surface and worked into the soil." This cautious advice is applicable to many crops. In allusion to *wheat, barley, oats*, it is further stated : "The employment of dung upon some soils insures the production of a good crop of corn, but upon other land it would, with equal certainity, destroy all our hopes of a satisfactory yield. When we are dealing with a rich clay, it is seldom that we can venture upon applying dung for corn, as it would cause a large growth of straw, to the prejudice of the yield of grain. When farm-yard manure is employed, it is almost always succeeded by a wheat crop, the use of dung for oats or barley being very exceptional." After forty years of experience, I still urge the use of Kelp, or the ashes of Sea-weed, as the best manure for wheat, producing the finest sample, and imparting such a silkiness and firmness to the straw as to render it fit for bonnet-making. In 1860, Dr. Voelcker (see Vol. XXI., 1859, page 286) made further important experiments with different top-dressings upon wheat, which last may be seen, Vol. XXIII., pages 16 to 22; and proposes, in soils in good condition, a top-dressing with $1\frac{1}{2}$ cwt. of nitrate of soda and 3 cwt. of salt, applied towards the end of March or the beginning of April—one of the best manuring mixtures that can be employed.

Dr. Augustus Voelcker, in his important experiments with different top-dressings upon wheat (in Vol. XXIII., 1862, pages 23 and 24) : Nitrate of soda alone gave not nearly so good a result as the same quantity of nitrate mixed with twice its weight of salt. This agrees perfectly with my experience of 1859; it should, therefore, be an invariable rule to mix nitrate of soda with salt when it is to be used as a top-dressing for wheat (page 30) : nitrate of soda and salt are best adapted to stiffish soils in good condition, and a specially prepared mixed mineral and nitrogenized manure to the soils which possess rather a lighter character or are naturally poor. On light land, I would recommend the following mixture, which I know, from experience, answers exceedingly well in an economical point of view : 1½ cwt. of nitrate of soda, 3 cwt. of common salt, 2 cwt. of Peruvian guano, and forty bushels of soot. The guano should first be passed through a fine sieve, and all hard lumps be broken up —a work which will be much facilitated by the addition of some sharp, siliceous sand to the lumps. When sharp sand is not at hand, perfectly dry and sifted coal-ashes or burnt clay may be used instead. The nitrate of soda and salt should be passed in like manner through a fine sieve; and as these salts are always more or less damp, and, therefore, difficult to sift, it is well to mix them previously with a dry substance in the same manner as guano. The next step is to mix these sifted and finely-powdered manures with a sufficient quantity of burnt clay or coal-ashes, to make up twenty bushels. These are finally mixed with the forty bushels of soot. Thus we obtain sixty bushels of a manure which will suffice for three acres.

The twenty bushels which have to be used per acre will cost about 25s., and, I have no doubt, will be found a very economical and useful top-dressing for wheat.

A. Voelcker (in Vol. IV., Part II., Second Series, 1858, page 397), "On the Causes of the Benefits of Clover as a Preparatory Crop for Wheat," gives an important notice to farmers, after a scientific research, which may be consulted with advantage (p. 420). Many years ago I made a great many experiments relative to the chemistry of farm-yard manure, and then showed, amongst other particulars, that manure spread at once on the land need not there and then be ploughed in, inasmuch as neither a broiling sun nor a sweeping and drying wind will cause the slightest loss of ammonia; and that, therefore, the old-fashioned farmer, who carts his manure on the land as soon as he can and spreads it at once, but who ploughs it in at his convenience, acts in perfect accordance with correct chemical principles involved in the management of farm-yard manure. Indeed, no kind of manure can be compared, in point of efficacy, for wheat, to the manuring which the land gets in a really good crop of clover. The farmer who wishes to derive the full benefit from his clover-ley should plough it up for wheat as soon as possible in the autumn, and leave in a rough state as long as is admissible, in order that the air may find free access into the land, and the organic remains left in so much abundance in a good crop of clover be changed into plant food. Again, when the clover-ley is ploughed up early, the decay of the clover is sufficiently advanced by the time the young wheat-plant stands in need of readily available nitrogenous food, and this being uniformly distributed through the whole of the cultivated soil, is ready to benefit every single plant. This equal and abundant distribution of food, peculiarly valuable to cereals, is a great advantage, and speaks strongly in favour of clover as a preparatory crop for wheat.

Professor Voelcker's further experiments on wheat, made in 1862 (Vol. XXIV., page 106).—A comparison of the preceding tabulated results suggests the following observations :—

1. Nitrate of soda, as in previous years, produced a considerable increase both in corn and in straw.

2. The larger application of nitrate of soda produced a correspondingly larger increase in corn.

3. In the third experiment, 2 cwt. of nitrate of soda and 4 cwt. of salt gave scarcely a larger increase than in the fourth experiment, in which 2 cwt. of nitrate of soda was used alone. This was also the case in my wheat experiments in 1861 ; whilst in the preceding years of 1860 and 1859 the addition of salt to the

nitrate of soda had a markedly beneficial effect upon the wheat crop. To show the commercial results, I have constructed the table (Vol. XXIV., page 108), of which I merely quote the two greatest profits over the unmanured plot : 2 cwt. of nitrate of soda and 4 cwt. of salt gave a profit of 3*l*. 15s. 1d., and 2 cwt. of nitrate of soda, 4*l*. 1s. 9d. Previously, it is said, the wheat is valued at 48s. the quarter, the price at which it was actually sold ; and the straw at 30s. per ton, as a usual selling price."

As regards economy, there can thus remain 'no doubt that nitrate of soda, as well as Peruvian guano, either alone or mixed with salt, may be used with great benefit as top-dressing for wheat—at least, on calcareous soils which, like our soils, contain an abundance of mineral plant food. Mr. Stratton, of Wakscourt, gave proof of this in 1862. He writes to Dr. Voelcker : " The plant of wheat was good, but it looked weakly in March. I, therefore, sowed in April nitrate of soda at the rate of 1½ cwt. per acre over the whole piece (three acres), with the exception of one land in the middle. At harvest the unmanured portion was accurately measured, as was the adjoining land ; and the produce was carefully kept separate and thrashed. The result was, without nitrate, 16 bushels per acre ; with the dressing, 36 bushels 1 peck. The straw was quite doubled in quantity."

Allusion has been made to Mr. Lawes' valuable report in 1851 regarding Mr. Keary's careful experiments on the Home Farm of the Earl of Leicester at Holkham, in Norfolk. In like view, that of cultivating wheat on the same land for several years by means of different descriptions of manure in succession, Mr. Lawes and Dr. Gilbert have carried out extensive trials both at Rothamsted (Herts) and at Rodmersham with the practice of those scientific gentlemen, by Mr. George Eley, at Rodmersham, about three and a half miles from Sittingbourne, in a field of three and a half acres, the soil being described by Mr. Eley as a "mixed clay upon a chalk sub-soil, lying from four to six feet below the surface." These experiments were carried on over a total period of six years, at the expense of Sir John Tylden, and a patriotic club of the good men of Kent—a pattern for every loyal Agricultural Society. The land was divided into seven plots. Those who desire to see the interesting details must consult the reports. The marked success is only here given. It will there have been seen that both mineral manures alone and ammoniacal salts alone yielded almost identically the same amounts of increase of corn over the first four years of the experiments at Rodmersham (Kent) as they did over the same years at Rothamsted (Herts), where wheat had been grown for a dozen previous consecutive years. The increase of straw by each of those manures, used separately, was, however, greater in the Kent experiments than at Rothamsted. The effect was altogether different when the mineral and nitrogenous manures were used together; the combination yielding an average annual increase of about twenty-one bushels of corn and twenty-two and a half cwt. of straw at Rothamsted, against only eight bushels of corn and twenty-one cwt. of straw at Rodmersham. Farm-yard manure (which is accessible to all farmers) gave, over the four years of its application, an average annual produce of about three bushels less dressed corn, and about eleven and a half cwt. less straw than the mixed mineral manure and ammonia salts; and about two and a half bushels less corn and about eight and a quarter cwt. less straw than the guano, neither of which would supply either silica or carbonaceous matter. This result is perfectly consistent with that obtained at Rothamsted and elsewhere. It is not to be concluded from this, however, that the farmer may with impunity grow large white straw crops by means of artificial manure without a due supply of farm-yard manure to the land at some period of the rotation. These extremely important experiments, how interesting soever to the scientific farmer, with capital at hand, I very diffidently submit, are not the safest practice for the great mass of farmers. Unless carried on with the same skill and caution, it might prove a losing business to continuously grow the same crops on the same land, and a too dearly bought experience to have abandoned the three or four other shifts which experience may have established to be the fittest for the soil and climate. Nevertheless, all honour to those patriotic individuals who investigate Nature in the vast unknown!

CHAPTER IX.

ON A CHANGE AND CHOICE OF SEED.

It is generally believed that an occasional, some say a frequent, change of seed is indispensable; otherwise the plant, soon becoming familiarised to the soil, loathes it, as it were, and consequently diminishes in produce. I am strongly inclined to believe that this is an erroneous idea; partly owing not only to negligence in the selection of seed from the finest of a crop, but also to a want of attention in the arrangement of succession, which I have before spoken of.

It is perfectly true that all plants become tired of one soil and of one manure. They, like the human race, have their appetites and loathings, and a person that would be forced constantly to eat the same sort of food, would not only infallibly sicken of it, but most likely suffer in his health. So it is with the cultivation of wheat, or any other plant. The best cultivator of Luzerne I have ever known, whose practice extended over forty years' experience, assured me that until he adopted the method of giving his land fresh food yearly, he never made it produce as he had since done. One year it was dressed with decomposed manure; the next, with ashes; the third, with salt; and the fourth, with lime.

I have applied this principle to wheat. That which is grown on land manured from the mixon one year, becomes seed for land prepared with lime; that again becomes seed for land dressed with ashes, then for land dressed with mixed manures, and so on, varying the food as much as possible; hence giving a good variety every chance of finding a new soil on each occasion. It may be objected that such a system could not be continued on a larger farm, where five or six hundred acres of wheat come into rotation. That may be true to a certain extent; but a little address and judgment, even on such a scale, by judicious subordination, would enable a farmer to surmuont the difficulty, as fifty acres kept in rotation on such a farm, solely for seed corn, even at thirty bushels the acre, would be the required quantity. So on a small farm, where only fifty acres of wheat would be cultivated, five acres, skilfully managed in the same way, might prevent the deterioration or degenerating of a variety suited to the soil and climate. It is sometimes difficult to replace a good and suitable variety, though it may have degenerated, as it is called.

Columella was so aware of the importance of procuring the choicest seed, that he observes, "I have this further direction to give, that when the corns are cut down and brought into the threshing floor, we should even then think of making provision of seed for the future seed-time; for this is what *Celsus* says: 'Where the corn and crop is but small we must *pick out all the best ears of corn*, and, *of them*, lay up our seed separately by itself. On the other hand, when we shall have a more plentiful harvest than ordinary and a larger grain, whatever part of it is thrashed out, must be cleansed with the sieve; and that part of it which, because of its weight and bulk, subsides, and falls to the bottom of the sieve, must always be reserved for seed; for this is of very great advantage, because, unless such care be taken, corns degenerate, though more quickly, indeed, in moist places, yet they do also in such as are dry.'"

This ancient, but most intelligent and accomplished, farmer and writer was thus fully aware of the importance of selecting the finest and choicest wheat for seed, evidently aware also, from the circumstance of his alluding to the heaviest wheat sinking to the bottom of the sieve, that the most farinaceous wheat was the most nutritious, and best fitted for the purpose of nourishing the young plant in its embryo state. Nor can there be a doubt but that the most plump, well-grown, and perfectly ripe wheat is the fittest for seed.

It has frequently puzzled me much to imagine upon what principle some writers have recommended for seed a sort of inferior grain, the refuse of a crop, after all the best had been sent to market. How a principle so entirely contrary to the whole economy of nature—which usually produces the finest progeny from the healthiest and most robust parents, the same being improved, or weakened, in proportion to proper or improper nurture and culture—could for a moment obtain, it is difficult to conceive; but it was merely argued that because a large quantity of sickly seed was sown, and that a portion of it grew, and produced a fair crop, it might be considered safe practice. Even from the finest seed, after five years of experiments, I am persuaded that for a crop, one-tenth of the best grain perishes, or is destroyed by birds, mice, or insects; but from some sorts which looked sickly, and were purposely tried, sown singly, grain by grain, I found that in a liver-coloured variety which, from the appearance of the ear, promised to be highly productive, though the grains were ill-grown, thirty-three grains out of seventy-two died—which induced me to discard it as being too delicate, its grains being poor and lean, though grown on a rich and well-prepared soil. Another variety, also from poor, ill-fed wheat, lost forty-nine grains out of sixty-two. A sample of Golden Drop, which I got at Mark-lane, tolerably well grown, had seven varieties in a handful, and thirty-four of these died, out of seventy-two grains. Whereas from other healthy plump grains of several varieties, only nine, ten, and twelve died, out of seventy-two grains of each variety.

Columella also entertained an idea regarding the degenerating of wheat, which is still entertained by modern farmers, quite erroneously in my opinion; the causes of which, according to my view of the question, will be explained in the succeeding chapter.

In one season the *Belle Vue Talavera* was so well-grown and plump, that of three rows of seventy-two grains each not one died; of No. 1 Dantzic, only three to four in three rows of the same number; and of No. 2, *Album Densum*, only eight from the same number died.

From one hundred and forty-four grains of a new white spring wheat—a very rare, hardy, and promising variety—only ten died.. Hence, with both farinaceous and productive habits I think I am also combining hardy qualities, selected from among forty or fifty sorts, which habits and qualities I am more or less acquainted with, as far as regards this climate.

My general observations lead me to believe that where wheat appears to grow lean and poor-looking, it should be discarded from the locality after a fair trial, say after the third year, as the second only might be the result of climate or the want of being naturalised to the soil.

The first trial should be made from seed of the best quality; if this fails after the third year, it evidently is unsuited to the soil and climate, and a new sort should be introduced.

It must be obvious that lean and shrivelled wheat is not so likely to nourish the young plant just starting from its embryo state into life, with a mere miserable skin of a parent to live upon, as the fine rich nutriment to be met with in a plump, round farinaceous grain, full of meal. As well might a farmer expect to have a fine, fat, skipping calf from a poor, lean cow, fed, or rather starved, on Dartmoor Heath.

CHAPTER X.

ON THE TENDENCY OF WHEAT TO DEGENERATE.

THIS term, "degenerate," is in common use among farmers, from a want of having duly reflected on the subject, and accepting for truth the traditions or sayings which become proverbial from father to son.

If I rightly understand the signification of the term, it should mean that the wheat has changed its nature; it has become of an inferior quality, less productive, and less suited to the soil than when originally sown. Now, having shown the very considerable difference of produce in various varieties—some producing nearly double what others do—it stands to reason that if a farmer procured what he used to consider a fine sample, apparently tolerably pure, and that a few grains, of a productive but coarse sort, were intermixed with it, say for the sake of argument, fifty grains in a bushel on the average, that this variety produced sixty grains to the ear, with an average of eight tillers to each grain; here would be four hundred and eighty grains, the produce of one single ear multiplied by the *fifty grains* in the bushel, or 24,000 grains in the produce of each bushel of an inferior sort in the crop, the following year. The second, or third year, if careful attention were omitted in the selection of the seed from the original sort meant to be produced, the crop would be thus almost *changed*, not *degenerated:* it would be no fault of the superior sort first imported, but wholly the consequence of neglect in not having preserved it pure, for the original sort would remain the same as regards quality, but diminished in quantity. So it will be, in a greater or less proportion, with each of these varieties, that lurk in a good crop, which they deteriorate in proportion to their inferiority, either in point of produce of meal or straw. This is the case even among the careful selections which I have made, for in the operations of thrashing, winnowing, or preparing corn by washing or pickling, with all the care imaginable, corn is of so small bulk that some stray grains, if several sorts are grown on a farm, will invariably lurk and get into the most pure crop. This I hold, under such circumstances, to be almost inevitable; but where only one or two good and suitable sorts are cultivated on a farm, mixtures ought to disappear altogether, and the stock continue pure as long as proper attention is paid. This should be done by methodical arrangement; first, by seeing the seed corn intended to sow down an acre or two, as future stock for a large farm, carefully selected by hand if necessary. That sown by a drill machine, with a double-distance between each sowing of the drill, to enable a careful person to reach from each side to the middle of the drill, when the wheat is ripening, to cut off any ears foreign to the crop. A guinea expended in extra labour in this manner would amply repay the farmer in the future beauty and produce of his crop.

When the sheaves are tied I further send a person round them, to see if all strangers to the crop are excluded from it.

All this may appear discouraging, but what success is to be obtained in this or any other profession (for I do not hesitate to call farming both a science and a profession), without mental application, added to the "*sweat of the brow*," in order to learn how to cultivate the soil with proper skill?

A very good farmer in the Lothians sent me a sample of wheat of his own growth—it had been intended for a white wheat, and was called so, but most of the white grains were ill-grown and poor; whereas a few grains of a red variety, mixed in the sample, were very plump and farinaceous, evidently marking that the degenerated or red sort, as it probably was considered, was that which would have insured a heavy, well-ripened, and remunerating crop.

I trust that the growing of seed corn for particular

localities may become a distinct branch of the Agricultural profession. I do not feel envious of those admirable establishments, the nursery-gardens of the kingdom, which hourly clothe the face of the country with new beauties, and refresh it with delicacies— the result of close and scientific investigation, extracting, like bees, sweets from every climate under the Sun, and naturalising them to a soil so foreign to many of their habits; yet I do hope to see a species of nurseries for wheat established in all parts of the Empire, and under every variety of our insular climate, where it will be known what sorts of wheat are best suited for its different soils, whether of clay, lime, sand, granite, trap, or other bases.

It must inevitably stand to reason that the fine white wheat which is grown on a rich fertile loam, suitably retentive of moisture, cannot be the proper sort to be sown on a poor black soil, such as Bagshot Heath, which of itself is incapable of retaining or attracting moisture.

But it will not be denied that if a red or coarse variety, equally productive as to quantity, though perhaps less farinaceous, could be grown on such a soil, it would be an end greatly to be desired, and of much national importance.

An observation which I made leads me to believe that such will be the result. In a piece of land which had been ill-prepared, and was poor and out of condition, a crop of white wheat had been sown; it scarcely grew three feet in height, but among it was a plant of fine, tall, rich brown wheat, with a large round, but rather coarse, grain. It proved a highly productive variety. <u>Had I happened to have sown the field with all such, instead of having had only twenty bushels per acre, I should probably have reaped forty.</u>

Surely the attainment of such results ought to be a matter of grave inquiry, as a means of increasing the national wealth. It is not my object, however, to write a treatise on political economy, but I shall not hesitate to point out what appears to me to be a legitimate and certain mode of augmenting the capital of the kingdom, by the means of husbandry.

The importance of the exact adaptation of plants, or their varieties, to particular soils, has been hinted at by medical men, who profess to have traced the origin of the cholera in India to improper food, or to the use of ill-grown and vitiated rice. There can be no doubt that if wheat unsuited to a particular soil be sown, the chances are that it will not be properly ripened, especially if in a moist or northern climate, where September or October weather may catch it; under such circumstances, the crop must be reaped, thrashed out, and perhaps sold at a low rate—at all events, somebody might have to eat it; so that an unripe, impure, deteriorated aliment is circulated, to the injury of some portion of society. Had the seed been such as suited the soil, the contrary might be expected: a well-ripened crop, enabling the farmer to pay his rent; and a wholesome nutriment being brought into the market. On one occasion a very beautiful-looking crop was sacrificed in the following manner. It was about the period when a good deal was written and circulated respecting the great advantages to be derived from cutting wheat while the grain was not fully ripened, as a means of considerably increasing the quantity of meal.

It was, therefore, reaped in an almost green state, while the thumb-nail could be pressed through the grain; the consequence was, that it shrivelled, and, I imagine, never dried, for when it was ground into meal, and prepared for baking, the dough would not rise, and the bread it produced was so heavy (absolutely lead-like and indigestible), that it was unfit for ordinary human stomachs, and nearly the whole crop was given to the pigs.

It will not answer to run into extremes in farming. If beginners deviate from the usual practice, let them do so with caution, and commence with small experiments, which, when established to be on correct principles, can be extended with safety.

Experience seems to have told that such a selection as above proposed has been attended to. It is satisfactory to perceive that a great number of farmers have hitherto made selections of varieties of wheat best suited to their own locality. For instance, the following sorts have all been tried by members of the Royal Agricultural Society of England in many counties, some in Scotland, and ably reported on in many cases. Numerically, 1, Brown Lammas; 2, the Clover, a brown wheat; 3, Golden Drop; 4, Whittington; 5, Snow-drop; 6, Browell; 7, Old Red Wheat; 8, Chidham; 9, Spalding; 10, Red Lammas; 11, Hopetoun; 12, Old Suffolk; 13, Talavera Spring Wheat; 14, Oxford Prize; 15, Browick Red; 16, White; 17, Nursery; 18, Scotch White; 19, Chaff Red; 20, Improved Lincolnshire White; 22, Hallett's; 23, Brown's Prolific; 24, Hunter's White; 25, Red Wonder; 26, Bristol Red; 27, Red Nursery; 28, Red Langham; 29, Woolly Ear White; 30, Victoria White; 31, Red Rostock; 32, Casey's White; 33, Niagara Red; 34, Clover's Suffolk Red; 35, Archer's Prolific; 36, Fenton White; 37, Berkshire; 38, Lewin's Eclipse; 39, Clutton; 40, Brown Chevalier; 41, Burrill; 42, Hardcastle; 43, Old Essex; 44, Pregglesham; 45, Ten-rowed Prolific; 46, Earl Toham; 47, White Dantzic Lincoln; 48, Dantzic Oxford;

49, Old Welsh White Lemon; 50, Mullybrack, Norfolk; 51, Pearl, Scotland; 52, French; 53, London Superior; 54, Royal Standard; 55, Baltic; 56, Kentish Long; 57, Britannia; 58, Buckland Toussaint, Devon; 59, Suffolk Thickest; 60, Buff Surrey. There are a vast many more valuable sorts in cultivation by name in the United Kingdom. However, these sixty are sufficient to establish the principle which was originally put forth in this little work—namely, to ascertain by experiment which might be the sort best suited to each soil and climate, of the most productive besides farinaceous qualities. The Scotch farmers are wisely careful to obtain the best or more prolific sorts from a South country.

In order to ascertain whether my view of the permanent characteristic of wheat, after thirty-six years of experience and experiment, was correct, I caused a square perch, twenty-two feet by twenty-two (ninety of which make up an English acre), to be sown in the following manner with my Belle Vue Talavera wheat of the original grain: The soil was prepared in the usual manner—dressed with lime and decomposed manure—as in ordinary farm culture. The seed was soaked twenty-four hours in brine sufficiently strong to float a potato, then drained off, mixed with dry sand and with powdered lime, for sowing ; two hundred grains, the produce of selected ears, sown one foot apart, in rows one foot wide, occupying half the perch. The other half-perch was sown with a pint of the same wheat as in field culture, in drills three inches deep, on the 26th November, 1870. This was reaped on the 29th of July, 1871, and produced thirteen pounds, of a very good sample, equal to thirty-nine bushels to the acre, of sixty pounds weight to the bushel. The former half of single grains, one hundred and eighty-four of which, out of the two hundred grains, was reaped three days later, and produced ten pounds ten ounces of a rather less ripened sample, equal to thirty-one bushels to the acre, of sixty pounds to the bushel.

The characteristics of this wheat have not altered ; an elongated ear on a very fine straw, rather delicate in habit, apt to be laid in high winds, owing to the weight of the grain, which is rather adhering to the ear. It is best suited to a sheltered and warm situation. I have grown fifty-two bushels to the acre, and twenty-seven pounds of its flour have produced thirty-five pounds fourteen ounces of bread of the finest quality. Nevertheless, I should not recommend it for general culture in exposed situations. It appears to me to be strange that farmers or experimentalists in furtherance of Agricultural science, have not constantly and earnestly sought for the bread-producing varieties of wheat, rather than being satisfied with the mere growth and produce of corn. I am now prosecuting a similar experiment with Chiddam's wheat. The space is enclosed with wire netting seven feet high to preserve it from birds.

CHAPTER XI.

ON THE DISPOSITION OF WHEAT TO SPORT.

HAVING doubted the general tendency of wheat to degenerate, I will now endeavour to show how such an accident may occur. From careful observation it appears that some varieties, if sown the same day, differ in their period of flowering, many days, even ten or twelve, intervening. Hence, a farmer who might be desirous of cultivating two or three sorts on his farm, by attending to this circumstance, would scarcely stand a chance of intermixing his crop, as fecundation could only take place at the time that each variety blooms.

He might further increase the difference of the period by sowing the earliest kind on the warmest exposition. Where the varieties flowered at the same period, there would certainly be danger of alteration in a future crop. The knowledge of the period of blooming of every variety should, therefore, become a science.

It is very extraordinary that some (sub-varieties they should be called) have a predisposition to sport, or to alter their appearance. A fine red sort

(No. 7), in the original experiment (see Table No. I.), was sown with the others, apparently pure; but, to my great surprise—even to that of Professor La Gasca, who witnessed the whole arrangement of it, and classed the sub-varieties himself—out of three hundred and fifty ears, the produce of forty-six grains, there were two hundred of the original sort, which were a red compact hoary or velvetty kind, twenty-one ears of a smooth red, eighty-six of a whitish downy appearance, and forty-three smooth chaffed white ears. It might be conjectured that the original or parent ear, having been discovered in a field of mixed white corn, had been impregnated by the pollen of four different sorts of wheat, which the peculiar conformation of an ear of wheat might admit. Professor La Gasca classed the original sort as a seedling.

Another and later instance of this propensity to sport I found in a Kentish downy seedling of an unusually square compact form, bearing a fine white plump round grain. I was anxious to propagate this, as it appeared so close and compact in its form that the wind was not likely to have much power on it. It was accordingly sown, but I had the mortification to find that it produced a great number of smooth ears, though there was little difference in the appearance of the grain; I therefore set that produce aside, and tried to raise it from a single ear again, but from 72 grains, whereof 13 died, eight ears were of a smooth sort, so that I considered it incorrigible, and have withdrawn it, as a sub-variety constantly liable to change.

The Talavera, flowering much earlier than any other, is sure to continue pure, unless stray grains happen to be accidentally mixed with it. No. 1, which I call Jersey Dantzic, flowers ten days later, and is very little disposed to change. I suspect the taller wheats are not liable to be impregnated by the shorter sorts, but the contrary to be the case. It is of consequence, therefore, to endeavour to keep all those varieties which are found to answer the purpose required as far apart from each other as possible.

One sort that I grew close to some others in the course of experiments, so far from having any affinity for them, actually exhibited a sort of dislike or shrinking from some of its neighbours. It occurred in a very raré sort of spring wheat, bearing white grains (most spring wheats bearing liver-coloured dark grains); this absolutely took a curve, even contrary to the prevailing winds, from a winter wheat planted fourteen inches to its left, and bent towards some rows of spring wheat which were on its right; this last, another variety, showing no predilection or dislike towards either of its neighbours. Hence, I am led to imagine that, from some unknown delicacy of habit, it loathed, as it were, the neighbourhood of the winter wheat, and leaned towards its summer neighbour. This was the more remarkable as the periods of flowering of the summer and winter wheats were not the same. I therefore conclude spring wheat may be sown with perfect safety by the side of winter wheat, without any fear of intermixture.

I hold it to be of paramount importance to ascertain and keep a note of the period of flowering of each variety to be cultivated on extensive farms, which will tend more to the keeping up a pure sort than any other method, care being taken also to cause the barn to be well swept as each sort is finally disposed of.

It may be of no small importance to be able to sow spring and winter wheats at the same time, for it must be clearly understood that many spring wheats will stand the winter as well as winter wheats, and as they would then invariably flower at different periods, it would be a certain mode of insuring pure crops, besides attaining another essential object—that of having flour, of a moist nature, from the spring wheat, to mix with the dryer flour of the winter variety.

That there is difficulty in keeping crops pure, no one can deny. Nevertheless, attention and care, with perseverance, will enable a farmer to keep a crop of wheat sufficiently pure for a length of years. The few varieties that may unavoidably insinuate themselves into it should be carefully removed.

CHAPTER XII.

ON THE EARLY HABITS OF SOME VARIETIES.

It has long been the practice with intelligent farmers to procure seed wheat from warmer climates, especially those in the North, to whom it is important to obtain seed that may ripen a fortnight earlier than that of home growth.

The chances are that such wheat, having the best and warmest weather to ripen in, will have attained its full state of maturity; hence, not only be the most productive in farina, but also the fittest for seed.

I have had occasion this season to satisfy myself by observation of the excellence of such practice. I sowed seven grains of the Victoria wheat grown on Dartmoor Heath; they were very poor and lean; however, five of them grew, throve, and ripened among my select varieties. They were sown on the 10th of November, in order to compare the produce and volume of their grain with some of the same sort, which were to be sown on the 29th of March following; they rose on the seventeenth day, were in ear on the 1st of June, were in flower on the 10th, and were ripe on the 23rd of July.

Those sown on the 29th of March were on a light soil in a warm position; they came into ear on the 19th of June, flowered on the 1st of July, and ripened on the 20th of August. The first of these two experiments establishes that it is a hardy variety, as it stood the winter perfectly; the ear and grain is also finer and plumper than that sown in the spring. The term *Tremois* wheat, however, does not apply to those climates which are not sufficiently warm to force the growth of corn so as to ripen it in ninety days, this having taken one hundred and forty-four to ripen. Two samples of seed wheat from the Cape of Good Hope, which had been sent by friends, as particularly fine samples, for seed, which they really were, led to some interesting observations. I was anxious to succeed in raising wheat from the Cape, as it has been questioned whether wheat which has crossed the Line would vegetate; this being stated in "The Farmer's Series, No. 74, of the Library of Useful Knowledge," Article, " British Husbandry," Chap. X., page 156: "Some fine species have lately been imported from the Cape of Good Hope and from Van Dieman's Land; but it was found, when sown on one of the finest farms in Bedfordshire, that it would not grow; and it is said, though we know not with what truth, *that scarcely any wheat is ever known* to vegetate in this country that had crossed the Line, unless particular care be taken to preserve it from the effects of the atmosphere."

Hence it became an object of no small interest to succeed in raising it. It was with great satisfaction, therefore, that I perceived both samples growing freely in November last.

In the spring their growth was quite different from that of any other wheat near them, whether from Dantzic, Poland, Carraccas, Essex, or this Island. It was much more upright, bushy, and of a lighter green, and trailed and tillered less. It put on also a rather sickly appearance, as if suffering from the cold. It came into ear on the 26th of May, six days earlier than the Carraccas wheat, but came into flower two days later, on the 12th of June, and only ripened on the 28th of July, five days later than the Victoria wheat, which had been sown the same day.

It is to be observed that there was much bearded or spring wheat among it, which appears, on first acquaintance, to have nearly similar habits as the winter wheats it came among, but seems to be very fine.

The sickly appearance alluded to above in the Cape wheat was indicative, doubtless, of a yellow description of smut, that appeared in it in June, which I had never observed previously to infest my wheat; it destroyed many of the grains, some of them being reduced to a mere shell, or skin, containing a small worm.

A most singular circumstance may be noticed here: I had sown sixty-three drills of this same seed from the Cape, on the 29th of March, in a field having a considerable slope to the Southward —a warm yet exposed situation. A great quantity of the seed perished, but all that rose had a healthy appearance, of a dark green colour, quite different from that sown in the garden; it came into ear on the 19th of June, flowered on the 1st of July, and ripened on the 10th of August. Not a single ear was infected with the yellow smut I complained of in the experiment made in the garden among my select varieties. Hence it is clear that this wheat from a hot climate, when sown in November on flat land, suffered much from the cold and wet, while the very same sample of seed sown so late as the 29th of February, on a warm slope exposed to the rays of the sun, found a genial and somewhat similar climate to its own, and succeeded perfectly. It is not unlikely that the produce of this last, sown with judgment, a little earlier, and in a warm position, may become a valuable importation, and preserve early habits for more northern climates. Some which was given me as *Kubanka*, a thin, liver-coloured wheat, which was exhibited before the Channel Islands Committee in 1835, turned out to be a spring or bearded variety; it came into ear on the 1st of June, flowered on the 18th, and ripened on the 10th of August. It does not tiller much, and appeared so like barley that I was doubtful what it should be; it was a perfectly pure sample, though much of it died. The Duck's-bill, a very productive sort from Kiel, in the Baltic, is said to produce meal fit only for pastry. It is the finest ear that I have seen. A cross with a variety producing a light dry meal would be highly advantageous. Its habits are late, as it came into ear on the 12th of June, and flowered as late as the 29th; it, however, ripened on the 6th of August. The Golden Drop, a fine, brown-eared variety, is equally late. This is a very farinaceous sort; probably one of the best of the red wheats, on which, as well as on spring wheats, I shall treat apart—my present observations being chiefly confined to white wheats, which are the first in order as to value.

CHAPTER XIII.

ON THE PROPERTIES OF SOME VARIETIES.

I HAVE stated the relative weight and fineness of quality of the varieties delineated in this volume.

It may be well to say a few words in respect to their relative value as to produce of straw. It is stated in the excellent work I have already quoted, at the Article " British Husbandry," Chap. X., page 154 : " The straw is generally reckoned to be about double the weight of the grain ; an acre, producing three quarters of wheat of the ordinary quality, may therefore be presumed to yield about twenty-six hundredweight."

If the results obtained by my experiments are of any value, the quantity of straw produced from a single ear of the best varieties, namely, No. 1, Jersey Dantzic, one of the best varieties, produced three pounds three ounces of wheat in round numbers, dropping the fractional parts, and three pounds nine ounces of straw, only six ounces more straw than wheat ;* No. 2, "*Album Densum,*" produced two pounds twelve ounces of wheat and eight ounces more straw than wheat ; No. 5, " *Coturianum,*"

---
* See Table No. 1.

six more straw than grain, and No. 8, "*Koeleri,*" four pounds four ounces of grain, and only *three* pounds thirteen ounces of straw. The next, No. 9, the Red compact, produced only two pounds nine ounces of wheat from three pounds fifteen ounces of straw—an excess of one pound six ounces of straw over the grain in the last sort; whereas in the former, No. 8, a most excellent and superior variety, there was an excess in grain of seven ounces over the straw. It must be obvious from these facts that, by a proper system of culture, wheat should be brought to such perfection as to produce more grain than straw, Nos. 8, 10, and 13 having done so; but I particularly allude to No. 8, from its being an exceedingly valuable variety in every respect, with the exception of retaining moisture in the ear a considerable length of time after rain, from its being velvet-husked, or downy.

The observation from the "Library of Useful Knowledge" may be perfectly correct as far as it regards ordinary husbandry, but it leads me to believe, what I have already ventured to state, that the proper culture of wheat is not yet thoroughly understood by a large majority of farmers.

It is a curious fact that the fifth of a pint of seed of the Dantzic variety, similar to No. 1, sown in drills about as thick as a drill machine would have sown it, Nos. 15, 16, 17, 18, and 19 should have nearly accorded with the statement, for, with the exception of No. 15, which produced only three pounds six ounces of corn from about "*two thousand*" grains, they produced *six pounds ten ounces*, or very nearly *double* the weight of straw; corresponding with the extract above alluded to—whereas row No. 1 of the very same sort, from only *sixty-one* grains, produced within three ounces as much grain, but little more than half less straw. These, surely, are startling facts, worthy the consideration of farmers.

The straw of No. 1 is of a beautifully white colour, very fine, but rather apt to lay in rich soils; the grain is tolerably tenacious to the husk, not much liable to shed. That of No. 2 is rather coarser and stouter; the grain is very tenacious in the ear. No. 5 has a short straw, white and slight; it is also little liable to shed the grain. That of No. 8 is still shorter, but fine, and excellent for fodder; indeed, they appear to be among the very best, as cattle eat them all greedily. As I have before observed, this last, being a hoary or velvet-eared variety, may not be suited for a damp climate, as it retains moisture for a considerably longer period than either of the former sorts, but on dry uplands it is highly productive, and valuable in every respect. In damp situations the smooth-eared sorts, both white and red, I apprehend to be the best. The Talavera, which I have raised from a single grain, has a slight white straw; it is rather apt to lay in rich soils, the ear being apparently too heavy for the stem; but a variety very similar to it, which was given me by Professor La Gasca, that was sown on a poor soil, came up very fine in the ear, though its not being above three feet high in the straw enabled it to carry its head upright. Should it continue to possess this quality in richer land, it will be a great improvement in the variety; this I shall be enabled to ascertain in future experiments.

Many valuable hints may be acquired with respect to raising new varieties from seed, and the mode of intercrossing them, by impregnating the female blossoms of one variety with the pollen or fecundating matter of the male organs of the other, which, if not done with some degree of care and attention, being a nice and difficult operation, may produce many varieties, of habits peculiarly liable to sport. I imagine that the only sure mode of preventing such an intermixture would be to leave only one female blossom on the plant to be impregnated, thus insuring a single variety of the precise quality required.

There can be no doubt that, with due attention, the practice can be established as satisfactorily as the success that has been met with by those who have attended to the intercrossing of geraniums, now grown of all shades and colours, almost at will.

CHAPTER XIV.

CLASSIFICATION.

THE attempt to class the varieties of wheat is necessary; it is a laborious and difficult undertaking, which should be performed by a more scientific person than the writer. But as no one has yet done so, as a branch of Agriculture, in those plain terms which may be intelligible, not to the botanist or scientific reader only, but to the great mass of farmers, I shall risk the trial for those sorts that are in usual cultivation.

I leave to botanists the seven species of *Triticum* named in that very useful work, Loudon's " Encyclopædia of Agriculture," also the attempt at classification that is made in Sinclair's very excellent book on Grasses, neither of these works explaining what I should consider to be the principal object in view —the nature and real qualities of each variety, as to their properties for making bread.

A gentleman who may be planting a garden is desirous of having peaches, figs, pears, grapes, apples,

L

even gooseberries, of particular seasons, flavours, qualities, and colours; these are all named, and so intelligibly classed, that if the nurseryman deceives him in one or two of them, he is set down as a person who is not to be depended upon; yet these luxuries which do not directly affect the real prosperity of the country, are perfectly well understood; but the nature of the most precious of all those plants, which one of the most profound writers has called "the only produce of land which always, and necessarily, affords some rent to the land," appears to have been overlooked—perhaps because it was so plentiful and so diminutive. If Dr. Franklin's adage, "Take care of the pence, and the pounds will take care of themselves," is true, it is not less correct to say to a husbandman, in the selection of his seed wheat, "Take care of the pecks, and the quarters will take care of themselves."

To render the classification of wheat well understood, it should be so clear and simple that any farmer should be enabled to state the precise variety he wishes to raise by applying to the seed merchant—a branch of business which should belong to the corn trade.

I should propose a classification as follows :—

BEARDLESS OR WINTER WHEATS.

Class 1. White Wheats, Smooth Chaffed.
,, 2. ,, ,, Velvet Husked.
,, 3. Red ,, Smooth Chaffed.
,, 4. ,, ,, Velvet Husked.
,, 5. Yellow ,, Smooth Chaffed.
,, 6. ,, ,, Velvet Husked.
,, 7. Liver ,, Smooth Chaffed.
,, 8. ,, ,, Velvet Chaffed.

BEARDED OR SPRING WHEATS.

1. White Spring Wheat.
2. Red Spring Wheat.
3. Yellow Spring Wheat.
4. Hoary Spring Wheat.

The sub-varieties should be given a number and name, which number should be first added to the local names given to each, for which one common name should be substituted.

ARRANGEMENT.

1st. The name of the wheat, and the particular soil and climate it may be suited for; the proper period for sowing it; whether it be liable to injury from drought, moisture, or frost, in its early or later growth; and its liability to disease.

2nd. The period of flowering or blooming and ripening.

3rd. The height and nature of the straw; whether it be white or dark-coloured, brittle or tenacious; if liable to lay in wet seasons, or otherwise; if fit for fodder, thatching, bonnet-making, or other purposes.

4th. Nature of the ear, whether compact or widely spread; its length in inches. This would, of course, vary in some soils, but it would be interesting to know such variations, the produce per acre.

5th. The colour of the grain (this will also vary with a change of soil); whether coarse or thin-skinned; whether round or oval, large or small; whether liable to shake out or not.

6th. Nature of the flour and bran, with their relative quantity.

7th. Whether the dough rises well or not.

8th. Quantity of bread made from a given quantity of flour; its colour; if of a dry or moist nature; and the length of time it will keep.

SMOOTH CHAFFED.

In Class 1.—*Nature and Habits.*—(*Table No. I.*)

PLATE III.—No. 1. *Triticum Hybridum Candidum Epulonum Leucospermum* " *La Gasca* "—No. 1 in the table—a variety from Dantzic; ear full and large, ranging from $3\frac{1}{2}$ in. to $4\frac{1}{2}$ in. in length. Grain, rather thin-skinned, large, roundish, hardy. Tillers well, blooms rather early, tall (4 feet 8

PLATE III.

Jersey Dantzic.

Triticum Hybridum.
Candidum Epulonum, of La Gasca.

Small Round.

Triticum Hybridum.
Album Leusum, of La Gasca.

J. LE COUTEUR *(after Nature).*

PLATE IV.

Triticum Hybridum.
Coturianum à Compactum,
of La Gasca.

Talavera   Belvuensis.

J. LE COUTEUR *(after Nature)*.

inches), tenacious white straw. Rather liable to lay in rich land, sheds if over-ripe, produces excellent white bread of a rather dry nature : 18 lbs. of flour have made 24 lbs. of bread ; has produced 52 imperial bushels of 63 lbs. to the acre.

PLATE III.—No. 2. *Triticum Album Densum* "*La Gasca*"—No. 2 in the table—I suspect it to be the *Froment Blanc de Hongrie* of the French ; ear compact, square, from $2\frac{1}{2}$ in. to $3\frac{1}{2}$ in. long. Grain small, white, round, and thin-skinned ; hardy, tillers well, blooms a day or two later than No. 1, tall (4 feet 8 inches), stout white straw, sheds little.

PLATE IV.—No. 3. *Triticum Hybridum, Coturianum à Compactum La Gasca, M.S.S.*, a seedling of 1832—No. 7 in the Table. Ear short and compact, not quite so square as No. 2, which it otherwise resembles externally ; from $2\frac{1}{2}$ in. to 3 in. long ; grain plump and oblong, rather coarser-skinned than No. 1 ; hardy ; tillers remarkably ; blooms rather earlier than No. 2 ; straw short and slight, 4 feet high, not at all liable to be laid ; sheds little, highly productive, having afforded 58 imperial bushels to the acre.

PLATE IV.—No. 4. *Triticum æstivum, Talavera Belvuensis.* Ear long, straggling, and pyramidal, from 4 in. to 6 in. long ; grain large, oblong and thin-skinned ; tillers moderately ; earliest to bloom, eight or ten days sooner than the three preceding sorts; straw tall, slight, and bending, and brittle if over-ripe; liable to lay in rich land; highly farinaceous.

In Class 2.—*Velvet Husked. White Wheat.*

PLATE V.—No. 1. *Triticum Koeleri; La Gasca,* 1832. Ear large, rather close; downy or velvetty; white, very plump, roundish, oval, thin-skinned grain; tillers remarkably; blooms rather early; straw 4 feet 4 inches to 4 feet 7 inches, very white and firm, not liable to shed, retains moisture from its huskiness, therefore should be harvested when dry; has produced 26 lbs. of superior white bread from 18 lbs. of flour, and has produced 55 imperial bushels of 64 lbs. the acre. This is the Kentish Downy or Rough Chaff, 1872.

Such is the sort of classification I should wish to introduce, not one in a dead or botanical language, intelligible only to men of science, but one in the mother tongue, which every farmer may comprehend, and by comparing his class-book with the crops, or varieties that are lurking in them, may ascertain which they are.

This is merely a first suggestion; time and further experience, guided by the experiments this little book may lead to, would prove the means of distinctly ascertaining and making known the habits and properties of all sorts of grain.

PLATE V.

CLASS 2.—VELVET HUSKED WHITE GRAIN.

1. *Hoary.*

Triticum Koëleri, of La Gasca.

J. LE COUTEUR *(after Nature).*

CHAPTER XV.

ON THE RELATIVE ADVANTAGES OF THE DRILL OR BROADCAST SYSTEMS, OR THICK OR THIN SOWING.

MUCH has been written on this subject which still appears debateable. My own observation leads me to believe that it rests mainly on the knowledge, skill, and long practice of the farmer. If a skilful and intelligent farmer has, for a long series of years, hoed, manured, and treated his land *so as to have* eradicated all the seed weeds from it, and it remains in so clean a state that nothing but the intended crop will germinate; then, indeed, I should say the broadcast system would afford the greatest produce. But if the case be with most farmers, as my own, that the land to be cultivated is loaded with the seeds of many descriptions of noxious weeds, then, I contend, the drill, or partly fallowing process, is that which is alone likely to enable the farmer to obtain a compensating return from his crops. I have observed a field of wheat sown broadcast in very good rich soil, so completely overrun with weeds, that, at the very lowest computation, two-thirds of it were lost. In every case where the ordinary means are adopted, whether the expensive process of hand-weeding or the much less costly mode of hoeing broadcast, it is attended with manifest risk if not most carefully and attentively performed, as any of the young tillers that may be drawn or cut will reproduce fresh ones, the ears from which ripen a fortnight or more, later, than those which were uninjured ; and the crop from such a mode of culture can never be in the most fit state of ripeness for harvesting.

By the drill process just before or about the period that the wheat is forming its coronal roots, which, from wheat sown on the 18th of January, I found, as may be seen by Plate II., to be on the 17th of April, there is ample time to have it lightly but carefully hoed, so that the weeds may be completely destroyed, and the coronal roots find a well-stirred soil to work in ; moreover, the plants, being in a free atmosphere between the drills so cleaned, which the weeds previously to their destruction breathed in common with them, have the whole benefit of the soil.

Those who desire to sow clover and rye grass in the spring will find it to be good practice to sow them a day or two before the first hoeing is given, as the same stroke which destroys the weeds mixes the grass seeds with the soil, which then take possession of it sooner than a second crop of weeds; but this mode, which I have found successful in regard to the future hay crop, is, I consider, at the cost of several bushels per acre on the wheat crop.

My own practice is to put my seed wheat into fresh water two or three bushels at a time, then stir it till all the light, injured, or sickly grains are floated or skimmed off; the grain thus cleaned is put to soak twelve hours in brine, made strong enough to float a potatoe; it is then put to drain, and is well dried with air-slacked lime; no smutty ears appear after such treatment. The land is prepared by two or three ploughings, and a dressing of lime, ashes, or some suitable manure, according to the change required in the food of the seed. The wheat is then sown with a five-row drill machine, in drills seven inches apart, at the rate of two bushels to two and a-half bushels the acre, after potatoes or parsnips.

One careful hoeing in April or May is then sufficient to enable the wheat to get the upper hand of its enemies, the weeds, for which purpose I use a hoe of my own invention, with a very narrow steel blade, not wider than a table-knife, with a stout blunt back and a very sharp edge, the sides being rounded off like some cavalry stirrups I have seen. The workman is thus enabled to place the back of the hoe against the very roots or tillers of the wheat, and thus scoop out any weed from them. In hoeing straight along the drills, the work is performed very speedily, as the round projecting sides of the hoe guide the labourer, and prevent his cutting the plants; the blade being so narrow prevents any accumulation of earth on the hoe, which glides or cuts through the dry surface with great ease and scarcely any resistance to the person using it. Women, or even children, can handle it with facility. My gardener has adopted it for all his drilled crops, finding it a safe, commodious, and very powerful instrument. The clover and grasses are sown immediately after the crop has been harvested, which has been found to answer remarkably well, though at the expense of one additional ploughing—a practice I have adopted, having observed it to be corroborative of Mr. Sinclair's experiments, who states in the "Hortus Gramineus Woburnensis," page 248: "I have sown the seeds of the same grasses in every month of the year, January excepted; and though much depends on the weather and state of the ground, the results were always in favour of the month of September and the beginning of August, and next to that, the middle or latter end of May, according as the weather was dry."

This principle is obviously in accordance with common sense; for in the first place the wheat crop receives the whole benefit of the manure which was intended for it without being deprived of any part of it by the grasses; the land also is, as it were, partially fallowed by the hoeing in the spaces between the drills, and is thus cleared and prepared for the grasses at the most propitious season of the year, according to the high authority just quoted; while the stubble that is lightly turned in is itself a manure for them, and keeps the soil open and light in a proper state for the young seedlings.

Fallowing for a whole season is altogether too expensive a mode to be adopted by those who pay a high rent for their land, as paring and burning, and the drill system, or a sort of half fallow, will answer the purpose equally well. From land in a very bad state, infested with couch grass, on one occasion, by means of paring and burning, previous to taking a crop of potatoes, which produced 34,800 lbs. of saleable potatoes the acre and with an after-dressing of forty bushels to the acre, of kelp or seaweed ashes, I raised forty bushels of fine wheat to the acre. One season I raised fifty-five, and on the previous season fifty-one bushels to the acre.

These are not mere assertions without proof, as a reference to my corn and miller's book would furnish all the details.

It may be seen what a perch of ground might be

made to produce, by multiplying the nineteen rows exhibited in the Tables by the produce of *No.* 8, *Koeleri*, which would give eighty pounds weight to the perch, or ninety bushels to the acre. Now, extraordinary as this may appear, I have no doubt that land, in a perfect state of tilth, and with seed suited to the soil and climate, may hereafter be made to bear that quantity.

Herodotus mentions an encouraging fact, which should lead farmers to hope, not, indeed, to rival the produce of wheat in Egypt, but greatly to increase their own. In his *Clio* it is stated: " Of all countries which have come within my observation, this is far the most fruitful in corn. Fruit-trees, such as the vine, the olive, and the fig, they do not even attempt to cultivate; but the soil is so particularly well adapted for corn, that it never produces less than *two hundred fold;* in seasons which are remarkably favourable it will sometimes rise to three hundred: the ear of their wheat as well as barley is four digits in size. The immense height to which Millet and Sesamum will grow; although I have witnessed it myself, I know not how to mention. I am well aware that they who have not visited this country will deem whatever I may say on the subject a violation of probability."

This elegant and authentic historian, who flourished

about 450 years before the Christian era, speaks of wheat producing two or three hundred fold. It is true the soil and climate of Egypt are both highly favourable to the growth of wheat, but the produce is not extraordinary, taking into consideration the fertile deposit left by the Nile, and magnificent wheat climate of Egypt, if compared with the produce from single ears of corn ; as No. 7, which produced 4 lbs. 4 oz. from 56 grs., reckoning 9,000 grs. to the pound, is a produce, between six and seven hundred, for one. Hence, may not British culture be hereafter brought to equal Egyptian produce?

"On the Advantage of Thick Sowing," by David Barclay, M.P. (Vol. VI., page 192, 1845): "The results of these experiments are very remarkably in favour of thick sowing, and particularly of the old broadcast system ; and if not conclusive against the doctrine of thin sowing, so strongly and, I may add, so ably advocated in the present day, should at least induce caution on the part of farmers before they depart from the practice of their forefathers."

In the "Report on the Wheat selected for Trial at Southampton," by W. Miles, M.P., and on other Wheats :—

"Drilled Wheats.—No. 1, Jonas' Prolific Seedling, 2 bushels per acre, produced 48 bushels; No. 5,

Fenton Scotch Wheat, 2 bushels per acre, produced 49 bushels.

"Dibbled Wheats.—No. 1, Not reported; No. 5 (the best), Fenton's, 2 pecks 1 quart per acre, 34 bushels, 1 peck, 2 quarts."

In this instance the dibbled wheats, as may be seen by reference to page 571, Vol. VI., 1845, were a failure.

"Experiments in Thin Sowing," by J. J. Mechi, Tiptree Hall, Essex, in 1845 (page 538, Vol. VII., Part 2): "Two fields of wheat were drilled, half with one bushel, twelve inches apart, half with two bushels, six inches apart. In both cases the produce was as nearly as possible equal, although the thickest sown *appeared* rather the best. *Thin* sowing should be *early* sowing on heavy land. Thin sowing somewhat delays the ripening of a crop, especially if sown on heavy land so late as November or December."

"On Different Varieties of Wheat and the Advantages of Thick Sowing," by W. Loft, Lincolnshire (Vol. IX., page 282): "In order that a correct judgment may be formed as to the sort of wheat and the quantity of seed best adapted to different soils. With this view, then, I venture to give you the result of two experiments made by me in the growth of wheat. The first was in 1844, and the second, last year (viz., 1847). The soil of this district—viz., the Lincolnshire Marshes—consists principally of a loamy clay, on a strong, tenacious clay sub-soil, and is generally what is termed a good wheat and bean soil. In 1844, I had planted in the same field twenty-six varieties of the best wheats I could procure. These were carefully put into the ground by hand, after a crop of rape eaten off with sheep. Eight of them were white wheats, the remainder red. In all the white sorts there was a considerable quantity of smut, two or three of the finest sorts being much the worst, whereas amongst the red three cases occurred, and two of those only very slightly affected with smut. The quantity of seed used was at the rate of 5 pecks per acre, and the average yield about 45 bushels 2 pecks the acre." It is stated further on that the marigold wheat in the two years produced the immense crop of from 56 to 57 bushels per acre. This result is at variance with the opinion of the advocates of thin sowing as to quantity of seed ; and indeed, I do not believe that any specified quantity of seed can be laid down for all descriptions of soil and climate ; practice and experience alone must be the guide. W. Miles, M.P., adds, in a note, "I feel convinced that very many circumstances, to be determined alone by the tenants of the respective farms, must decide the quantity of seed to be sown on the respective localities"—an opinion in which I heartily concur.

"On the Proper Quantity of Seed for Wheat," by R. B. Wolfe, Woodhall, near Newport, Essex (Vol. XI., 1850, page 184).—Mr. Wolfe had made a report to the Royal Agricultural Society in 1848 on this subject, and now adds the detail of cultivation, which may be seen at p. 185, *ibid*, with the important result : " I have this year acted upon the conclusion I have come to, and drilled all my wheat (about eighty acres) with six pecks of seed, and at eight inches apart, and up to this time I am perfectly satisfied with the promise. It was remarkable that on four modes of sowing the produce per acre was between five quarters two bushels two pecks and five quarters four bushels per acre, and the weight per bushel from 61½ lbs. to 63 lbs."

The "Lois Weedon" mode of growing wheat in alternate strips is alluded to merely to notice that, even with the careful trial given to it by Mr. Lawes and Dr. Gilbert (page 582, Vol. XVII., 1856), the system was given up by them. Indeed, such a departure from ordinary good culture is only likely to be successful when the experimenter happens to possess the skill, patience, and industry of the originator. This view seems to be borne out by the following passage: "A great number of intelligent agriculturists have visited the 'Lois Weedon' Farm, and, after an inspection of the crops growing on the plans there adopted, have generally been satisfied that the produce has been what the published accounts had stated it to be. Yet it is somewhat singular that those who have endeavoured to follow the directions given *on other soils* have generally been unsuccessful." It is fair to add that in Vol. XVIII. of the Journal, page 30, Mr. Smith affirms that the experiment conducted by Mr. Lawes and Dr. Gilbert was ill carried on, and a deviation from his system, and, therefore, a failure. Nevertheless, it would seem to be one very hazardous for the generality of farmers. And it is only fair to draw attention to the Report of John A. Clarke on the "Lois Weedon System of Wheatgrowing with Horse Tillage" (Vol. I., Second Series, Part I., page 73 and on), in the South Lincolnshire "Marsh" country (page 79): "My experiment simply proves that *several paying wheat crops can be grown, one after the other, without any manure, provided the land be in fair wheat-growing order at the beginning.*" Mr. Clarke concludes an interesting and very clear statement with his conviction: " I shall be told that an extension of wheat culture is not advisable, because roots, clover and cattle crops, have of late years

M

answered better. But what can the wheat crops that do not pay possibly have to do with MY wheat crops, which will pay? The entire case rests upon the low cost of *production by my method in comparison with the cost of a wheat crop in ordinary farming.* I raise two good wheat crops in succession for 5*l.* 10s. per acre each (every source of outlay included), and at the same time, and for the self-same money, I am fallowing and cleansing the ground in readiness for roots or other of the third year's crops. Can any other system show an economy of expenditure like this?"

In Vol. VI., Second Series, 1870, pages 299 to 301, a remarkable and telling experiment upon wheat, barley, and swedes, by Earl Bathurst and other members of the Cirencester Chamber of Agriculture, reported by Professor Wrightson, of the Cirencester Royal Agricultural College, may be consulted to advantage. Here wheat alone is alluded to.

"WIDE DRILLING AND TILLAGE EXPERIMENTS UPON WHEAT.—The usual width of drilling wheat being about nine inches, it was resolved (1) to omit every alternate row, leaving a space of eighteen inches between the rows; (2) to omit two drills, and leave two, making a space of twenty-seven inches between double rows, nine inches apart; (3) to omit two drills and leave two, forking the interspaces during the summer; (4) to attempt the cultivation of carrots or potatoes between wheat-rows arranged as just described; (5) to try the effect of firmly pressing land with the foot in winter and spring."

These experiments were carried through, in the year 1869, with great care, by three skilful farmers, and at the Royal Agricultural College Experimental Farm. The summary at page 309 is not a little instructive. Such are the results of wide drilling and interculture obtained in 1869. In one case there was a remarkable increase of wheat and straw in connexion with a saving of one bushel of seed per acre. A second case gave an increased amount of straw per acre, and was thought up to harvest to promise a greater yield of corn; strict weighing, however, revealed a deficiency, probably due to mildew. A third series gave a slightly diminished yield upon land which had borne a barley crop the preceding year, and was consequently in low condition. Lastly, one of the four series gave an unequivocal answer in favour of continuing the usual system. It is a somewhat remarkable fact that all the experiments agree in condemning deep interculture between wide-drilled wheat. This has already been stated as an observed fact both in 1865 and 1869.

I take occasion to add that my own experience shows that too deep hoeing or culture necessarily disturbs what I have found termed as the "coronal roots," and therefore checks the growth of the wheat from its seminal roots, leading no doubt to debility of constitution and, mav be, to mildew, or smut, or weakly growth.

CHAPTER XVI.

RESULT.

By the evidence of Mr. Jacob, before the Select Committee on Agriculture, in 1833, whose authority is unquestionable, the average consumption of wheat in the United Kingdom was then about thirteen millions of quarters, and the average produce per acre, of England and Wales, about twenty-one bushels. This, for the sake of argument, I assume to have been that of the whole Kingdom, though it will somewhat overrate it for Ireland and Scotland; then, deducting the average importation of wheat since the year 1828, or a million and a-half of quarters, they had at that period about four million four hundred thousand acres in wheat annually.

From the circumstance of some portion of the country producing more than that average, I will suppose the land under cultivation for wheat to be five millions of acres.

Now, assuming the average price of wheat, forty years ago, to have been fifty shillings the quarter, it will readily be conceded that any means which could enable the farmer to raise one quarter of wheat—nay, half a quarter—more per acre, would not only be a great individual advantage, but a very large increase of the national wealth. A nation is a great family, and whether it be merely a portion of the great family—a family of Rothschilds, for instance, who are enriched by the intelligence, activity, and perseverance of one individual, or every individual, who, by the application of the same energies, is enabled to increase his own income—it is still so much increase of the national wealth, augmented in the ratio of the number thus actively employed.

It follows, if the mode I suggest, of raising wheat suited to each soil and climate, be strictly adopted, it may reasonably be expected, in the course of three or four years—such is the amazing productiveness of wheat—that the farmers in every district in the country will be supplied with suitable seed to suit its soil and climate, when an increase of one quarter per acre may reasonably be made to take place. Even more than this increase has occurred on my own farm, where three quarters per acre was formerly the average, but has now gradually increased, in three years out of four (one year's crop having been sacrificed to an experiment), from three or four to six quarters per acre. Hence, assuming the increase to be only one quarter per acre instead of the two or three which have taken place on my farm, that increase on five millions of acres, at fifty shillings per quarter, would present an annual augmentation to the national wealth of twelve million five hundred thousand pounds.

But this would not be the whole advantage gained. It is further stated by the same respectable authority that one million and a-half of quarters had been imported from abroad between 1828 and 1833, which may have been purchased for about two millions sterling; or, in other words, the English farmer at that period lost that sum of money yearly which he might have received for his wheat, but which was sent out of the country, and paid to foreigners. Again, these differences are merely calculated on the wheat. It is necessary to take into calculation the increase also in the quantity of meal that will accrue when the system of classification and the knowledge of the properties of each variety of wheat is attained. Although these illustrative comments relate to a period so far back, yet they are equally applicable, as an illustration, to the present, having reference to our future productive efforts.

I have shown that eighteen pounds of good Dantzic and Rostock flour only made twenty-three pounds of bread, also that eighteen pounds of a farinaceous variety of my own growth have made twenty-six pounds of bread. Here we have an excess of three pounds of bread on eighteen pounds of flour, or of one-sixth, from two superior sorts of meal, and I shall rest satisfied to make my statements from these —though I am convinced, were I to make them from flour taken from the average mixtures which furnish the flour that is eaten all over the Kingdom, the increase would be greater.

Let us assume that a bushel of wheat averages forty-eight pounds of both kinds of flour of that sort called "Seconds;" hence, if a superior sort of wheat be made to produce an increase of eight pounds of bread on every bushel, here would also be an increase of one shilling per bushel on ninety-two millions of bushels, or of four million six hundred thousand pounds a-year, being a general increase of value in the produce of wheat and flour to the amount of sixteen million nine hundred thousand pounds sterling, to which may be further added the sum that is annually paid by Englishmen to foreigners for corn, or two millions more, being a total increase of eighteen million nine hundred thousand a-year. I shall expect to be told that these are mere idle and vain speculations, quite theoretical and visionary; but I claim for consideration experiments of forty years, and the facts that I have been enabled to deduce from them. I readily admit that, to obtain the vast result I appear to jump at, a large and apparently unmanageable machinery would have to be put into motion, as well as the consentaneous action of, as it were, a whole people. But if only half—nay, a quarter—of the result is attainable, it is surely worth the attention of the Government as well as of the whole body of Agriculturists. It is not a system of harassing and vexatious taxation that I am advocating, to endeavour to relieve the country from a portion of the burdens which overcharge it; but a course of regular, slow improvement, sure and infallible in its result, acting steadily upon the best feelings and individual interests, requiring only a regular system, guided by one firm and powerful mind to put the machinery regularly into play.

It is not surely because the suggestion is simple, though new—perhaps I might add comprehensive—that it may not educe eminent and lasting benefits to the entire family of man. I am satisfied with pointing out this as one of the means to relieve the Agricultural interest, without going into further details, feeling persuaded that when the application of my principle shall have extended to red and yellow wheats, and spring wheats also, on neither of which I have yet treated, but have made many experiments, to be published hereafter, it will be seen that I have much underrated the mark. This proper adaptation of seed to particular soils will have the effect of diminishing the risk of the farmer—will therefore increase the demand for labour, and lead to an augmentation of the rate of wages.

The application of the principle is universal. I have therefore already sent some select samples to Persia, to North America, and to the West Indies; I only wish it to be given a fair and patient trial. It is in the proper and general application of it that the adage, "Union is power," will be found. Had I the means to set the machinery in motion, the result would be infallible after the third or fourth seasons. It must also be kept in mind that these results are calculated upon fair average crops, not on the differences which may exist between some of the best and some of the worst varieties, that I have set forth in the tables annexed to this book, nor on the extremes between crops in general cultivation.

If such were the case, the results would be far more considerable, as the difference between the best red wheat and the most inferior sort is greater than the difference in the white varieties. I shall further show that the produce and value of spring wheats is various, should the hints I have thrown out have been deemed worthy of attention.

In the report of "Recent Improvements in Norfolk Farming," by Clare Sewell Read (Vol. XIX., 1858, page 274), we are told that the next observable improvement is one of far greater moment. It is the increased productiveness of the *wheat crop*. Competent authorities assert that this district now grows *a quarter of wheat more per acre* than it did fifteen years ago. Another striking feature is the *great extent* of wheat which is now grown. A few years ago hardly any was sown after a root crop, but it is now almost universal to plant wheat after mangolds, and to sow a large portion of the turnip-land with it as well. The reasons for this change are, that wheat will bear high farming better than barley, is not so liable to be affected by unpropitious seasons, and on some soils will produce as much per acre. There is also another advantage, that the clovers, trefoils, and saintfoine—but especially the latter—grow much better with wheat than with barley. The wheat seldom lodges; its straw is stiffer, grows more upright, and readily admits the air. Having been planted some time before the seeds are sown, there is a firm seed-bed, with enough fine mould to cover them without burying them too deeply, as is frequently the case when sown on well-pulverised barley land (p. 297). The effect of this rise on the farming of Norfolk was a subject of general remark, and it so happened that in 1853 and

1854 the agricultural statistics of this county were collected; and the value of such tables is shown by their furnishing such facts as these: *that in 1854 there were 13,089 acres more wheat than in the preceding year, 7,594 acres less of bare fallow, and nearly 10,000 more bullocks kept in the county.* It is, further on, observed: "Statistics and figures are dry things, but are nevertheless very useful. Comparisons, if they are not always odious, are seldom pleasing, and so but one will be attempted. It is simply this: That in 1854 there were 267,000 more acres of wheat and barley grown in Norfolk and Suffolk than in the whole of Scotland; and the county of Norfolk alone produced 1,290,373 more bushels of wheat than all the land north of the Tweed. It is further stated that in 1805 the quantity of wheat sold in Norwich Market amounted to only 25,422 quarters; and in 1843, was increased to 124,872; and in 1857, to 168,739 quarters—a clear proof of very successful farming and increase of produce."

Mr. W. Wright, on the improvements in the farming of Yorkshire (Vol. XXII., Part I, page 112), states that on well-drained and properly-managed farms the produce of wheat varies from 36 to 40 bushels per acre; in some instances a higher estimate may be taken; while 20 to 24 bushels is the yield on those less cultivated or ill-managed. Few changes have been made in seed-wheat since the last report, though a greater quantity of the white sorts is grown than formerly.

Mr. H. M. Jenkins, in his report on some features of Scottish Agriculture, Vol. VII., 1871, page 160, (No. 7 Wheat): "Mr. Murray, at East Barns, who is a first-rate farmer, and cultivates wheat after potatoes and pulse, describes the mode of culture, which is not very different from that in the North of England. Rather less than two bushels of 'rough chaff,' or woolly wheat, are sown in drills from the 22nd of November until the end of December. One horse-hoeing is given where weeds appear. A top-dressing, of a mixture of 1 cwt. each of nitrate of soda and guano, is put on broadcast in April, when the wheat plant is fairly growing. The white crops are usually cut by machine. The best Scotch farmers *are very particular about their seed*. Mr. Murray generally gets wheat every year from *the South*. 'Last year (1865) the wheat crop at East Barns produced sixty bushels per imperial acre, but this year (1866), from the influences of the season, probably will not yield more than forty bushels. The average yield is from forty-eight to fifty bushels, weighing from $64\frac{1}{2}$ lbs. to 65 lbs. per bushel, and occasionally somewhat more.'"

At Fenton Barns Mr. Hope has the land steam-ploughed, with a deep furrow, about the end of

October or beginning of November, and, in the course of a week or two, is sown with two bushels of Fenton wheat per imperial acre. When well up, it is harrowed and rolled, and then generally Dutch-hoed by hand. The average produce was from five to six quarters per imperial acre.

Downhill, near Girvan, Ayrshire (p. 177, "*Wheat*") —" As the turnips are drawn, the land is ploughed to a depth of not more than five inches. *White* wheat, *Archer's Prolific*, is sown." As the result is not given, I conclude the extract.

At Holmston and Friarland (p. 185) the potato-land is ploughed, with a shallow furrow, in October. Wheat is sown in drills if the land is in good order; a broadcast sower is used on heavier land. About two bushels of white wheat, woolly rough chaff, or sometimes red chaff, is sown per acre. No result given.

CHAPTER XVII.

CONCLUSION.

THE Author may probably be excused for publishing the following letter, addressed to the Central Committee of the Agricultural Society of Great Britain and Ireland, in which will be seen a portion of his early efforts in Agricultural improvement at a period when its prospects were anything but bright. And it was not until the advent of the Royal Agricultural Society that the prospects of the farmer, founded on correct systems of tillage, taught and persistently advocated by the present "Journal of the Royal Agricultural Society," began that steady and successful rise in thrift and prosperity which now reigns in the farming interest. This happy state of things has been mainly brought about by entirely discarding party politics from the actions of the present Society, which weakened and ultimately ruined the power of their predecessors, and which was forcibly predicted by the Author at the time of their formation, should party politics be permitted to influence discussions purely agricultural.

"100, Quadrant, 20th December, 1835.

"My Lord and Gentlemen,

" Having been requested, by a resolution of the Central Committee of the Agricultural Society of Great Britain and Ireland, held on the 17th instant, 'to furnish a statement showing the advantages to be conferred on the Agricultural interest generally by the establishment of an experimental farm in the immediate vicinity of London,' I engage in the task with some diffidence, but with great pleasure.

"It may be pardonable, previously to my entering on my subject, briefly to attempt to win the confidence of my brother farmers, to whose impartial consideration these observations are particularly directed, by showing that the humble individual who unexpectedly addresses them for the first time, has some claims to it, having for the last eighteen years been ardently engaged in Horticulture and Agriculture; and though an Honorary Secretary to an Agricultural Society, it is not in name only, as he has earned premiums in fair competition for the superior culture of wheat, growth of new potatoes from seed, new mixed artificial grasses; for the ntroduction of new implements of husbandry, and for stock.

" The most ready mode of proving the utility of an institution is by a statement of analogous facts, the result of experience. In July, last year, having read, in a French Agricultural publication, an account of an Experimental Farm and School at Coetbo, in Brittany, about 300 miles from my residence in Jersey, I visited it in the hope that it would be useful to the Society of which I am Secretary.

"It is situated in a beautiful and fertile country, well-wooded and watered, but cultivated by the 'Breton' farmers just as their forefathers tilled it two hundred years ago. The College Farm appears like a garden in a smiling wilderness, so far as culture goes. I rose at four in the morning in order to witness the whole course of labour in this interesting institution.

"There were from eighty to ninety students, under the superintendence and tuition of a Director, a Professor of Agriculture and Agricultural Chemistry, a Veterinary Surgeon, and an Agricultural Implement-maker.

"At half-past four they took a slight repast, and as the clock struck five, all were employed—some in harnessing the oxen and horses, others in carting out and properly disposing the implements in the field; others set to hoeing, others weeding, some ploughing, some hay-making—in a word, to the various labours of the season.

"The School is divided into working parties of

ten; at the head of each is a steady young man of experience, called the 'Decurion,' who directs the work of his party. In all difficult operations, a regular farming labourer is at hand to perform them, but such is the ardour and perseverance of the youths, that they rarely allow any difficulty to arrest their progress. The duty of one decury, or ten, is to dress, feed, and litter the cattle* with as much regularity as a cavalry corps dress their horses, also to keep the farm-yard in order. Thus all, in turn, are made acquainted with everything connected with a farm, whether in regard to horses, oxen, cows, pigs, or manures. These last are made and husbanded with the greatest care, the mixons being formed of sweepings, leaves, and weeds that had not seeded, in alternate layers with stable manure.

"The draining of the stables and straw-yard run into a tank, to be pumped out when required as liquid manure, which is the best, most portable, but least known in this country.

"The learned Professor M. Donker, who is an admirable practical farmer, as polite and as communicative as he is learned, complained that he had not sufficient manure. I urged him to burn the underwood and decaying timber of the large adjacent

---

* At Coutray thirty cows are kept on a farm of 20 acres.

forests, through which wide roads were cut, which would enable him to obtain an inexhaustible supply of ashes—the best of manures, either for turnips or wheat—the cartage of ashes being easy, and the quantity required to dress the land not great—in which he entirely coincided.

"At nine all come in to their duties, when they write remarks on the various operations of the morning. From eleven to twelve is the breakfast-hour; from twelve to three is time for recreation and study, which embraces, for the first class, questions of the following nature : 'This farm of 600 acres, one-eighth of which is always to be in beetroot, is to be divided into the most eligible rotation of crops. Show the most profitable course, and describe the nature and chemical properties of the soil in each field ; the proper manures to be applied to them ; the quantity of seed required for the crop ; its culture, by previous ploughings, by after hoeing or weeding ; the cost and labour, and the probable return.'

"The plan of farming given by some of the youths would have done credit to an experienced farmer, and demonstrated clearly that, though theory alone in farming is an absurdity, the combination of practice with scientific acquirements will soon effect a great amelioration in the Agricultural world. From three to seven, they prosecute their labours in the fields, being eight hours' work in the day. They then come in for dinner. At eight the Director receives the report from every Decurion of the day's work of his party of ten. He then orders the work for the ensuing day, giving a concise lecture on the subject when necessary to the proper culture of any unusual crop. A library of Agricultural works is open to the students till bed-time—a quarter past nine.

"The greatest order and regularity prevails in this admirable establishment, which is supported by the French Government, and by voluntary contributions. There are two students from forty departments of France, besides a few more who pay for instruction.

"Some of them had been in the learned professions of law, medicine, and civil engineering, who having inherited estates, and being desirous to superintend and cultivate their farms, came to the School to learn husbandry, farm-account keeping, the mode of rearing and feeding cattle, and all rural pursuits. The uniform—a blue smock-frock, with a straw hat and red ribbon—contributed to give an air of rustic cheerfulness throughout the whole establishment.

"The crop that appeared to me to be most carefully cultivated was beetroot, in drills, which produced per acre about 750 lbs. of fine sugar, selling at 10d. per pound as fast as it could be manufactured. The potato crop was fine, very well horse-hoed, and perfectly clean.

"The wheat crop was good, much better than that of the 'Breton' farmers around, but foul with weeds, from not having been made in drills, which I recommended in future, until the weeds were extirpated from the soil. Indeed, I ventured to urge the propriety of having all the crops in drills for the same reason. The Swedish and other turnips were also fine and clean.

"There were, besides these principal staple crops, experimental crops of nearly 300 varieties, which it is unnecessary to enumerate, though some may become of paramount use to the farmer, such as the giant or red clover, *Trifolium Incarnatum*, which is an admirable supplementary crop when the turnip crop has failed. I strongly urge farmers to try it, on a small scale first. It may be sown as late as September, and furnishes a prodigious quantity of food in April or May, producing the finest butter possible if given to cows.

"The students attend to the culture of these crops, study their nature, properties, and their effects on cattle, which are daily—nay, sometimes hourly—noted.

"In turn they are present at all veterinary surgical operations, either on horses or horned cattle, and an explanatory lecture, one of which I witnessed, forcibly impresses on the minds of the students the nature and cure of the disorder.

"The Professor of Agricultural Implements, for thus he must be termed, demonstrates mathematically the points of greatest or least resistance in the construction of all instruments and ploughs, all sorts of which, from the primitive plough of the Lyonese, a mere beam fifteen feet long with a hook at its end, to the improved Norfolk or Scotch swing ploughs. Most modern implements were to be seen here—the Flemish binot, new harrows, dibblers, drills, horse-hoes, winnowing machines, turnip-slicers, chaff-cutters—all made up in the College workshops, in many instances by the students; any such as display a decided taste for mechanics, carpentry, or even smith's work, being allowed to indulge it under the eye of the Professor.

"Here, then, were a number of intelligent, active, and enterprising youths, all ardent in the pursuit of that knowledge which is the fiat of the most High, collected from every quarter of their beautiful, fertile, and extended country, imparting to each other a knowledge of its local wants, its various products, its agricultural manufactures and commerce; all anxiously occupied in the inquiry, what might be most useful and beneficial to fill and replenish their fertile soil—all desirous to convey to their respective districts the knowledge thus acquired. These youths, on their return home, would naturally preserve reciprocal ties of friendship with those whom they might never meet again, but whose correspondence on subjects relating to husbandry and the products which they might exchange would cement those ties.

"Can any reflecting mind deny that such an institution must prove eminently useful to an Agricultural country? The truth is, that our intelligent and active neighbours have at length perceived and anticipated that to act in detail and as a divided body, is not the means to attain great results; they have, therefore stepped into unity of design a day before ourselves.

"The kindly feeling towards an Englishman which husbandry generated in these young men, was truly delightful and impressive.

"It was no longer the averted eye and scowling brow, auguring war and insult, which I witnessed not twenty years ago, but that primitive honest feeling of barter expressed in these terms: 'What will you exchange with us for the new products we shall raise? You will give us your hardware, earthenware, laces, and manufactures, in exchange for brandies, wines, and fruits, which you cannot grow in your climate.' Such sentiments, generally diffused, will do more towards perfecting the amity between these two great nations, whose mutual interest is peace and commerce, than a hundred formal treaties.

"Having shown, I trust, the manifest advantages of an experimental farm on the other side of the Channel, I proceed to show that it was high time for that class of persons, among the most useful and intelligent, the farmers of this great country, instead of carrying on experiments in various corners of the empire—experiments which, how laudable soever, lost half their value, by being insulated and comparatively unknown, being confined to certain limits—to rise, united in object and design, in order to collect and condense the fruits of all such experiments, sow the seeds of such knowledge in one grand focus, and then scatter it abroad with a liberal hand.

"The Board of Trade is an office, acknowledged by the Legislature, especially to protect the interest of commerce and manufactures; but the Legislature acknowledges no such Board especially to protect the Agricultural interest—the origin of both the others.

"But the Central Committee of your Society, supported by your individual and joint interests, will soon, it is presumed, have its due preponderance, though without directly possessing the means for obtaining information which an office of the Government would possess ; information of vital importance, as appears by the evidence of Mr. Jacob, before the Select Committee on Agriculture, which sat in 1833, and was adverted to by that Committee, showing that 'if the bad harvest of 1816 were unexpectedly to arise again, followed by a second bad harvest, there might exist such a deficiency of wheat as could not be supplied by all the world ;' and the Committee came to the conclusion, 'That that increased supply from Ireland does not cover the deficiency ; and that in the present state of Agriculture the United Kingdom is, in years of ordinary production, dependent on the supply of wheat from foreign countries.'

"The price of wheat for the last five years, as stated in 1833, notwithstanding several deficient crops, has not in the average exceeded 61s. 8d. per quarter ; the highest price within the same period was 76s. 7d., the lowest 51s. 3d.

" ' *Steadiness of price, which is conducive to settled habits, and forms* the *basis of all fixed engagements,* is *the primary object never again to be overlooked;* and your Committee cannot fail to remark that there has been, coincident with the present system of corn laws, a *steadiness* in the price of corn, of which there has been rarely, if ever, an experience in any former period of equal duration; and as during the same period there has been a very considerable difference in seasons, and in the actual amount of corn produced, it is but just to ascribe to the *present system* a great degree of that *steadiness of price* which has unquestionably prevailed.'

" I am not exactly aware whether the *present system* which the nexisted, is the system now, but one thing appears clear, that the *steadiness of price* has strangely vanished; its fall from the lowest quotation of 1833, 51s. 3d. in two years, being about 15s. per quarter. Hence, instability of price having fallen on the country since that period, some further inquiry ought surely to be made on the causes of this extreme depreciation; so that inferior lands can no longer be cultivated with any prospect of a return. The Committee further stated : ' On the whole, it must be admitted that the difficulties are great and the burdens heavy which oppress the landed interests; but contracts, prices and labour have a strong natural tendency *to adjust* themselves to the value of money once established, and it is hoped that the balance may be restored which will give to the farming capital its fair return ;' and further on, in conclusion, ' Your Committee avow their opinion that hopes of *amelioration* in the condition of the landed interest rest rather on the cautious forbearance than on the active interposition of Parliament.'

" From this it would appear that the agriculturists must rather trust to their own exertions than hope for any relief from the Legislature, which has so recently been occupied in making twelve thousand nine hundred and three questions, which, with the replies, occupy 617 pages, on the causes of agricultural distress. It appears, therefore, doubtful, whether any legislative enactment could speedily relieve those heavy burdens which unhappily oppress agriculturists; the various interests of the State requiring to be so nicely balanced and adjusted, and being so closely interwoven, that any concession made to one might be detrimental to the others. Their ultimate interests are the same, for in all cases of successful industry, either in manufactures or commerce, the first step usually taken by the individual who may have honourably risen to affluence is to identify himself with the soil by the purchase of an estate; and what does he then become? One of ourselves, a farmer!

" But the first and most legitimate step towards relieving the farming interest is to unite in one great body, steadily to examine all the bearings of the question affecting its interests—not by merely calling out for help like the carman in the fable, but by putting a shoulder to the wheel; by rousing energies which have long lain dormant, by inquiring into each other's wants, by the introduction of new plants congenial to the soil, by the application of capital to the growth of new crops, by a rapid exchange of commodities—the harbinger to prosperity, which steam communication and railways will facilitate; by pointing out to the farmers that the soil is not cultivated to its extent, by clearly exposing that if he grows a crop of weeds in addition to the intended crop, it is just so much produce taken from his capital and given to waste. This holds good with pastures as well as with crops; if nothing but nutritious herbage were grown, another head of cattle, or more, would be reared on every farm in the Empire; while the increase of stock would be in proportion to the superior culture of the soil."

I have suppressed the last pages of the First Edition, as they principally urged the establishment of a model experimental farm, several of which have been established in various parts of the country.

In this Second Edition I have endeavoured to condense as much as possible the information which might be useful to young farmers from the volumes of the "Journal of the Royal Agricultural Society of England," especially that relating to the culture of wheat.

To those gentlemen from whose works extracts have been made, grateful thanks are offered. They were intended to convey to young farmers safe, practical hints by the most able agriculturists.

I cannot conclude without again most urgently impressing upon my brother farmers the imperative necessity of growing wheat crops from the best selected species of grain which shall give the least quantity of bran and the greatest quantity of meal, as, by timely care and watchfulness on this important culture, the grain, in the cereal wealth of Great Britain, cannot but be reckoned by millions sterling. In the untoward event of a protracted war, such labour might be of the highest political value.

www.ingramcontent.com/pod-product-compliance
Lightning Source LLC
Chambersburg PA
CBHW021733220426
43662CB00008B/837